Kierkegaard's Dancing Tax Collector

Kierkegaard's Dancing Tax Collector

Faith, Finitude, and Silence

SHERIDAN HOUGH

OXFORD
UNIVERSITY PRESS

OXFORD
UNIVERSITY PRESS

Great Clarendon Street, Oxford, OX2 6DP,
United Kingdom

Oxford University Press is a department of the University of Oxford.
It furthers the University's objective of excellence in research, scholarship,
and education by publishing worldwide. Oxford is a registered trade mark of
Oxford University Press in the UK and in certain other countries

© Sheridan Hough 2015

The moral rights of the author have been asserted

First Edition published in 2015

Impression: 2

Published in the United States of America by Oxford University Press
198 Madison Avenue, New York, NY 10016, United States of America

British Library Cataloguing in Publication Data
Data available

Library of Congress Control Number: 2014960020

ISBN 978–0–19–873999–9

Printed and bound in Great Britain by Clays Ltd, St Ives plc

For Christian

Preface (or: Cheerful Expository Warning)

'Preface': yes, the face before the facing, the whisper to the audience, the exhortation to the orchestra before lights dim and music swells.

Just as well, in this case, because this project has some odd structural features, and the reader needs to be ready to spend some time within its narrative frame, and the portrait of one character in the Kierkegaardian bestiary that thus emerges. But 'framed portrait' is far too static a notion; rather, this work is an 'existential-phenomenological' investigation of this singular Kierkegaard character (whom we will meet in the Prelude).

And what is an 'existential-phenomenological' investigation?

It is 'existential' in its pursuit of the issues that human beings are constitutionally called to address. A Kierkegaardian account of human being, and the demands and concerns that are part of our human lot, will be elaborated in what follows. This investigation, as it focuses on one notable character, is also 'phenomenological': what is it like, *really like*, to move faithfully through the world, given our human constitution? Here I take my cue from Husserl, who commands us: 'zu den Sachen selbst!', *to the things themselves*. The term 'phenomenology', when reading Kierkegaard, is perhaps a contentious one; here it should be heard in its most primordial sense: my exploration of the life of faith, and the person so living it, is focused on what 'faithful comportment' can, and cannot, reveal to us. In this sense this study is 'regional phenomenology':[1] we will be focused on the 'movements'

---

[1] I borrow this useful term from George Pattison, who questions attempts to read Kierkegaard's *method* in a comprehensively phenomenological manner: historically, phenomenological projects (as seen in Hegel, Husserl, and Heidegger) have, as he puts it, 'global ambitions' that seek '. . . a unification of the whole domain of experience and knowledge' (2002: 84). This project's 'regional' approach is happily free of such designs. (Cf. Merleau-Ponty: 'the opinion of the responsible philosopher must be that *phenomenology can be practiced and identified as a manner or style of thinking, that it existed as a movement before arriving at complete awareness of itself as a philosophy*. It has been long on the way, and its adherents have discovered it in every quarter, certainly in Hegel and Kierkegaard . . .' (1962: viii.)

solicited by faith, and the phenomenon of a particular way of being in the world.

Of course, the way that the world *is*, or is 'available' to a person (to use the language of contemporary philosophy of mind, the 'affordances' of a person's environment),[2] has everything to do with the condition of the person in question. 'Condition', for Kierkegaard, is surely an ontological designation: for the aesthete, the world is a venue for (unsuccessfully) satisfying one's cravings; for the ethical being, the world is a terrain to be mapped by reflection, articulation, and choice (endlessly); for the religious person, the world is the site of suffering that must be embraced through confession of sin and the knowledge that one is, 'before God, always in the wrong', a realization which demands the practice of active love. Notice that these are very different environments: a person seeking to satisfy an urge will be engaged with the human domain in a way that the ethical deliberator can only pity; on the other hand, the religious supplicant understands that the ethical task of getting it right is never done, and surrenders herself into the embrace of a loving God.

All of these ways of 'being-in-the-world' (more about Heidegger and such locutions momentarily) have a task, and each has opportunities and abilities that the others lack. In each sphere, the world is structured by a life-commitment that makes particular undertakings available, and others not. Of course, the target of human development is not any one of these 'spheres' or 'stages' in life; in the Kierkegaardian scheme the ideal 'condition' is that of 'faith', the ultimate and highest way of worldly engagement: for the faithful person, *everything is available*. (What this expression can actually mean is the subject of this book.)

But the language of 'highest' surely betrays the worldly demeanor of Kierkegaard's only depiction of a knight of faith, the fellow dreamed up by the author of *Fear and Trembling*, Johannes de silentio, a man who 'looks just like a tax collector'. (Yes, now that we have identified our celebrity-quarry we will not make him wait in the wings until the Prelude.) This 'tax collector' (so-called, for now) is a person of sturdy gait, absorbed in the unfolding moment, taking pleasure in,

[2] See J.J. Gibson (1979); cf. Susanna Siegel (2010: 130–1).

remarkably, *all things*: clearly, de silentio (and, obliquely, Kierkegaard) intends for the reader to observe the phenomenon of faith. A faithful person has powers that the aesthete, the ethicist, and the religious practitioner do not (not to mention the human beings who have yet to set out on the path to selfhood): the faithful tax collector finds his quotidian environment infinitely abundant, significant, and the cause for joy, from moment to moment. How can this be?

Of course, enlightened beings always seem strange to everyone else. Socrates famously could not be seduced or made drunk, and he went to his death with uncanny cheer; Siddhartha Gautama, upon becoming the Buddha, could cause harm neither through thought, nor speech, nor deed, nor could he be the victim of physical violence or mindless insult.

Consider these two examples of enlightened 'world-navigation': both are the culmination of considerable thought and practice that turns on a conception of what a human being *actually* is, a view shorn of conventional assumptions, one that is thus able to direct how best to fulfill that understanding of our human legacy. An ontological picture, once adopted, always makes existential demands. For the Buddhist, the true realization of the 'selflessness' of all things is made manifest in the refusal of grasping attachment to the passing scene; for the Platonist, the innate contents of the intellect must be dialogically recollected: once knowledge is achieved, a person moves through the world with discernment, able to see what is real beneath the shiny distractions of mere appearance.

Kierkegaard's ontology is no different. The account of human being he develops by means of his seventeen (or so)[3] pseudonyms—each describing some aspect of his respective aesthetic, ethical, and religious frameworks—establishes what is, and is not, available to the person navigating by means of the relevant coordinates. It is a developmental picture, and the life of faith is its fullest flowering. The silent, joyful perambulation of de silentio's faithful person is thus of considerable existential-phenomenological interest. Indeed, this 'existential-phenomenological' approach has both descriptive and diagnostic

---

[3] —depending on how you count them: more about these voices in the First Movement.

elements: if we have a good picture of our 'being in the world', then we can stake some claim about how best to live.

On the Method (of Reading Kierkegaard)

I should also be clear that my 'existential-phenomenological' account is not in any way opposed to a religious, or indeed specifically Christian, reading of Kierkegaard's corpus. Far from it. Clearly, any responsible reading of these texts begins with the fact that Kierkegaard is a Christian thinker who seeks to illuminate what it means to live as an *actual* Christian (and not, of course, simply as a member of Christendom). Kierkegaard clearly believes that Christianity speaks to our human condition—Christianity provides an account of human nature, and thus how best to negotiate the world we occupy, in much the same way that Plato's metaphysical account of the tripartite self, and the immortality of the intellect, is crucial for understanding what a fully realized human life will look like for Plato.

I will also confess that I read Kierkegaard comprehensively. The way of life afforded in each sphere of existence can only be seen from within that perspective: true enough, but the issues and difficulties of each are not utterly discrete from the concerns of the others. The pursuit of pleasure, the demands of deliberation and choice, the surrender of oneself before a loving God—each of these has a vast network of connective tissue, and sometimes the tug of one possibility can only achieve motility through a change in perspective. For example: as I will argue in what follows, the aesthete chases what he takes to be 'pleasurable', but only the faithful person has access to 'ongoing pleasure' (again, making sense of this remark is the task of this book). This project is thus not a 'post-modern' hop through the various spheres of existence, but a cumulative (sometimes retrogressively, at others retrospectively so) investigation of what the life of faith promises.

As for the very notions of 'existential' and 'phenomenological': I had better say a word about the usual suspects. (In fact, I've already mentioned two of them, Husserl and Heidegger.) We might begin by considering two of Kierkegaard's true descendants, Heidegger and Sartre. Heidegger's *Sein und Zeit* contains much that is recognizably Kierkegaardian (such as the 'idle talk' engaged in by the 'Public' and

'the call of conscience'; more of these in the First Movement);
Heidegger, however, is certainly in no hurry to acknowledge Kierkegaard's
influence;[4] in fact, Heidegger sets out to ontologize Kierkegaard by
rejecting the religious, individualizing dimensions of Kierkegaard's
work. Sartre's work is also deeply Kierkegaardian: the Sartrean picture of the structure of the self (in *L'Être et Le Néant*) as the opposition of
'facticity and transcendence' is surely a one-dimensional rendition of
Anti-Climacus's three-fold set of 'relata' that describes the human
situation in terms of opposed capacities (again, more about this in
the First Movement). Sartre's ideas of avoiding 'bad faith', acknowledging the 'self' as a condition always in the balance, and, above all,
the importance of freedom—all of these notions are first worked out in
Kierkegaard's corpus.

This investigation will, on occasion, make use of Heidegger (and
other existential philosophers, such as Simone de Beauvoir), but only
in terms of their considerable *debt*: and, here again, the concept of
'debt' is one that is important to both Kierkegaard and Heidegger.
Much has been written about what these existential thinkers have
used, distorted, obscured, and simply pilfered from Kierkegaard's
work; unfortunately, some of these accounts use Kierkegaard's work
as a mine for helpful nuggets, bits that necessarily anticipate the later
greatness of Twentieth Century figures (and beyond). Here I am not
interested in either approach (particularly the latter). This project is
focused on one Kierkegaardian figure, and one story-line, and so my
use of other moments in the history of philosophy is guided by what
use I can make of them in telling my Kierkegaardian tale. Plato and
Hegel will need to appear, of course, as well as thinkers in the
phenomenological and existential tradition: everyone will have their
say when they can elaborate on a particular puzzle or theme; however, this work will not be otherwise concerned with what they have
done (or failed to do) with their Kierkegaardian inheritance (interesting though such questions always are). In this arena, Heidegger and
Sartre are particularly prone to usurp the philosophical limelight; on
this occasion they will not.

---

[4] As Roger Poole puts it, 'Heidegger, struggling with Husserl for the effective
leadership of the phenomenological enterprise, remorselessly ransacks
Kierkegaard...' (1998: 52).

Nietzsche is indeed a special case in this crowd of historical fore-bears and descendants. His oeuvre—a canon as brief as Kierkegaard's is vast—bears many curious and uncanny Kierkegaardian resem-blances. Nietzsche did not get a chance to read Kierkegaard before his final, debilitating illness (other than bits gleaned from the later work of Bishop Martensen), but he shares Kierkegaard's disgust with 'Christendom', as well as his fascination with the tricks and traps of the human psyche. I will sometimes appeal to a Nietzschean perspective to elaborate on Kierkegaard's interpretive agenda.

Tuning Up

So: consider this a 'musical experiment' in the key of Kierkegaard. No noodling here, or unnecessary jazz riffs; instead, I will develop a melody-narrative focused on one enigmatic figure in one of Kierke-gaard's most important works. This narrative has an arc: the conclu-sions we draw at the end of each section will be revisited and revised as our picture develops. And thus my initial 'expository warning': this is not a book to dip into by way of the index. Conclusions drawn in one section may be denounced in the next; one depiction of how things are will give way to another. This is a plea for the reader's narrative indulgence. Kierkegaard's corpus lends itself to a universe of readings, so count this as one tale among many. I intend to tell you a story—my own, of course—but one that draws directly from the words of Kierkegaard's own voices (and from Kierkegaard himself).

Respectfully,
SH, LTC

House lights down, please. Curtain up.

Acknowledgments

The importance of gratitude is a central issue in Kierkegaard's thinking, and one that is writ large in my own existential concerns. I am hereby delighted to celebrate the mentors and friends who have made this project possible.

Every book has a taproot in the past, and indeed this one began to develop during my undergraduate years at Trinity University; thanks to Lawrence Kimmel and Peter French for encouraging me to find my own way in these multifarious texts. As a graduate student at the University of California, Berkeley, I had the great good fortune to study with Hubert Dreyfus, whose passion for Heidegger's existential phenomenology has inspired students for decades. My encounter with Heidegger has motivated my thinking about many philosophical debates, and my understanding of both Nietzsche and Kierkegaard is informed by the debt that Heidegger clearly owes to each. Thanks to Bert and Geneviève for many years of philosophy and friendship.

This book first took shape during my tenure as NEH Professor of the Humanities at Colgate University; I had the opportunity to complete an initial draft, and—best of all—to try some of it out on my students and colleagues in both the classroom and in a public lecture. The Colgate Philosophy Department is simply wonderful; special thanks to Maudemarie Clark, for her brilliant scholarship and wicked wit. Here in my home department at the College of Charleston, I am grateful to have ongoing, enthusiastic conversations about my work with my colleagues, whose philosophical projects are often somewhat distant from my own.

After several years of thinking and writing about Nietzsche and Heidegger, I returned to some earlier questions about Kierkegaard. I was fortunate to find Robert Perkins, the founding editor of *International Kierkegaard Commentary*, who encouraged me to pursue these issues in print. When I became particularly focused on *Fear and Trembling*, I was delighted to discover not only Sylvia Walsh's Kierkegaard scholarship, but also her careful, elegant translation of *Fear and Trembling*; this book makes use of the Walsh translation. Thanks to

Cambridge University Press for permission to use these passages from *Fear and Trembling* (© 2006). For my forays into the Danish language, I am indebted to the expertise and patience of Margaret Cormack; thanks also to Baroness Louisa Bille-Brahe, whose love of the Danish language has brought a number of Kierkegaard's nineteenth-century idioms to life for me.

Over several years, ideas at work in this book were road-tested across the globe as invited papers. Many thanks to Jay Garfield and the Smith College Philosophy Department; Chen-Kuo Lin and the Philosophy Department of National Chengchi University, Taipei, Taiwan; Kuan-Min Huang and Academia Sinica, Taipei, Taiwan; and Romulus Brâncoveanu and the Philosophy Department at the University of Bucharest, Romania. I have also presented some of this work in conference settings: some of these thoughts appeared in a keynote address at the American Philosophical Association in December, 2006; in a session of the American Academy of Religion in November, 2011; and at Brigham Young University in November, 2013. I was delighted to read from my work at Kierkegaard's 200th Birthday Celebration at the University of Copenhagen in May, 2013. Early, less elaborated versions of some material in Movements One and Four have appeared in *International Kierkegaard Commentary* (vols. 15, 18, and 23); thanks to Mercer University Press. In drawing a comparison with Nietzsche's account of the self, I have made use of ideas first explored in *Nietzsche's Noontide Friend: the Self as Metaphoric Double*; thanks to Penn State Press. Wendell Berry's 'Poem XII' appears in the book with permission, © 2010 Counterpoint Press. Thanks to Princeton University Press for permission to use these translations: *Either/Or 1 & 2* © 1987; *Eighteen Upbuilding Discourses,* © 1990; *Two Ages: the Age of Revolution and the Present Age,* © 1978; *Stages on Life's Way,* © 1988; *The Moment and Late Writings,* © 1998; *Upbuilding Discourses in Various Spirits,* © 1993; *Without Authority,* © 1997; *Works of Love,* © 1995.

Many wonderful people have befriended this book. Tom Perridge of Oxford University Press has been a thoughtful and compassionate editor. George Pattison has offered wise, illuminating comments about this manuscript. Fellow travelers have provided all manner of intellectual and emotional sustenance: thanks to Camelia Cercelan, Veronica Coseru, Ombretta Frau, Blaine Garson, Elizabeth Herring, Barbara G.S. Hagerty, Elizabeth and Robert Sharf, and Robert

Zaretsky. Thanks to artist Richard Hagerty (who, as it happens, is a fan of Kierkegaard) for the painting that graces the cover of this book. My philosophical friendships have sustained me through many years of thinking and writing about these issues; thanks to Jennifer Baker, Deborah Boyle, Andrew Burgess, John Davenport, Michael Della Rocca, Georges Dreyfus, Jay Garfield, Todd Grantham, Karsten Harries, Ned Hettinger, Larry Krasnoff, Glenn Lesses, Ulrich Meyer, Edward Mooney, Jonathan Neufeld, Richard Nunan, Marcia Robinson, Jane Rubin, and Mark Siderits. Special thanks to Susanna Siegel, for the philosophy as well as the poetry, and for the delights of sustained correspondence. As always, love to PL, and to FG.

My grandmother, Mary Margaret Griffis Cordell—who attended the University of California at Berkeley in 1919—was a keen reader of Kierkegaard; my grandfather, D. Glen Cordell, became a Presbyterian pastor later in life, and wrote a seminary thesis on both Kierkegaard and Jonathan Edwards; their interest in this strange Dane is surely now in part my own. Phyllis and Vernon Hough have patiently listened to many iterations of these ideas, and their ample curiosity and fondness for philosophical talk has made this a much better book (and me a far better person). Thanks to them both for a lifetime of love.

Heartfelt, ardent thanks to my fellow philosopher, colleague, and spouse, Christian Coseru. Our ongoing conversation is an enduring pleasure, and I am utterly grateful for his marvelous, witty erudition and generosity of spirit. He wears his many languages and specialties—from phenomenology, to philosophy of mind, to Buddhist epistemology—with loveable ease. Christian is the finest dance-partner on the philosophical floor that anyone could wish for, and the depth of my gratitude to him, and for him, must be indicated with love's profound silence.

Table of Contents

List of Abbreviations

CA   *The Concept of Anxiety*, trans. Reidar Thomte in collaboration with Albert B. Anderson. Princeton: Princeton University Press, 1980.

CI   *The Concept of Irony*, trans. Howard V. Hong and Edna H. Hong. Princeton: Princeton University Press, 1982.

CUP   *Concluding Unscientific Postscript to 'Philosophical Fragments,'* two vols., trans. Howard V. Hong and Edna H. Hong. Princeton: Princeton University Press, 1992.

E/O   *Either/Or*, 1–2, trans. Howard V. Hong and Edna H. Hong. Princeton: Princeton University Press, 1987.

EPW   *Early Polemical Writings*, trans. Julia Watkin. Princeton: Princeton University Press, 1990.

EUD   *Eighteen Upbuilding Discourses*, trans. Howard V. Hong and Edna H. Hong. Princeton: Princeton University Press, 1990.

FT   *Fear and Trembling*, trans. Sylvia Walsh. Cambridge: Cambridge University Press, 2006.

JP   *Søren Kierkegaard's Journals and Papers*, ed. and trans. Howard V. Hong and Edna H. Hong, assisted by Gregor Malantschuk. Bloomington and London: Indiana University Press, (1) 1967; (2) 1970; (3–4) 1975; (5–7) 1978.

PC   *Practice in Christianity*, trans. Howard V. Hong and Edna H. Hong. Princeton: Princeton University Press, 1991.

PF   *Philosophical Fragments* and 'Johannes Climacus', trans. Howard V. Hong and Edna H. Hong. Princeton: Princeton University Press, 1985.

PV   *The Point of View for my Work as an Author*, trans. Howard V. Hong and Edna H. Hong. Princeton: Princeton University Press, 1998.

R   *Repetition*, trans. Howard V. Hong and Edna H. Hong. Princeton: Princeton University Press, 1983.

SLW   *Stages on Life's Way*, trans. Howard V. Hong and Edna H. Hong. Princeton: Princeton University Press, 1988.

SUD   *The Sickness Unto Death*, trans. Howard V. Hong and Edna H. Hong. Princeton: Princeton University Press, 1980.

TA   *Two Ages: the Age of Revolution and the Present Age*, trans. Howard V. Hong and Edna H. Hong. Princeton: Princeton University Press, 1978.

TM   *The Moment and Late Writings*, trans. Howard V. Hong and Edna H. Hong. Princeton: Princeton University Press, 1998.

UDVS   *Upbuilding Discourses in Various Spirits*, trans. Howard V. Hong and Edna H. Hong. Princeton: Princeton University Press, 1993.

WA   *Without Authority*, trans. Howard V. Hong and Edna H. Hong. Princeton: Princeton University Press, 1997.

WL   *Works of Love*, trans. Howard V. Hong and Edna H. Hong. Princeton: Princeton University Press, 1995.

Every good and every perfect gift is from above, and comes down from the Father of Lights, with whom there is no change or shadow of variation. According to his own counsel, he brought us forth by the word of truth, that we should be a first fruit of his creation. Therefore, my beloved brethren, let every man be quick to hear, slow to speak, slow to anger, because a man's anger does not work what is righteous before God. Therefore put away all filthiness and all remnants of wickedness and receive with meekness the word that is implanted in you and that is powerful for making your souls blessed.

—The Epistle of the Apostle James, chapter 1, verses 17–21

If a person were permitted to distinguish among biblical texts, I could call this text (James 1:17–21) my first love, to which one usually (*always*) returns at some time; and I could call this text my only love—to which one returns again and again and again and *always*.

—Kierkegaard, journal entry, August 1855

1

Breathless Confessional Prelude

How and Why I Fell in Love With the Tax Collector

This is a love story. And, as with all profound loves, there is a mystery at its heart.

No, I am not in love with Kierkegaard the writer: what could *that* possibly mean? Magister Kierkegaard, tireless creator of lengthy works by various—and very different—pseudonymous authors: who is *he*, anyway? And to be smitten with his maddening hall-of-mirrors multifariousness, the duplexity of even his most straightforward voices? No, not at all and never. Anyone captivated with Kierkegaard's authorship, taken whole, must immediately rent out a vast estate of many rooms, filled with every imaginable human (and some non-human) manner of prolixity: Christian brothers and love-struck women, town sentinels and mermen, talking birds and worried lilies, fashion designers and judges, seducers and apostles.

Readers familiar with Kierkegaard's textual mansion will already know that Kierkegaard denies having built, or even owning, a huge part of it. He famously makes the following claim at the end of *Concluding Unscientific Postscript*:

> In the pseudonymous books there is not a single word by me. I have no opinion about them except as a third party, no knowledge of their meaning except as a reader, not the remotest private relation to them ... Therefore, if it should occur to anyone to want to quote a particular passage from the books, it is my wish, my prayer, that he will do me the kindness of citing the respective pseudonymous author's name, not mine ... (CUP, 627)

And let us remember: Kierkegaard's so called 'pseudonymity' is a complicated affair. Yes, many of his works are signed by someone else, but that pseudonymous author is only the first cry in a chorus of characters. What about all the other voices,[1] many of them writing in the first person, all of whom are also passionately (and often aggressively, even transgressively) providing the contours of their particular way of life? Surely the 'indirect communication' (as Kierkegaard calls it) must include this entire parade of personalities, each of them with their own peculiar way of being in the world.

—But as I said initially, this is a profession of a long-standing and curious kind of love. Since my very first reading of *Fear and Trembling* I have been taken with a character-sketch provided by one of Kierkegaard's pseudonyms, and *his* own marvelous (and silent) meditation on the very frame and nature of human existence. There. I'm stuck on a fictional character, imagined by a fictional author, who was created by that infinitely clever Master of multiple vanishing points and kind-of-poet religious author, Søren Kierkegaard. How are we to negotiate *that*?

My devotion to a fictional imagining of one of Kierkegaard's pseudonymous authors needs a narrative, one that will rely on thinking about the claims of many of those other voices, and certainly the voice of Kierkegaard himself. This book is an account of that journey, as I find my way towards what is for me (and perhaps only for me) the heart of Kierkegaard's life project.

Who, then, is this pseudonym, the creator of the object of my affections?

His reticence names him: Johannes de silentio, John of silence. But Johannes, for all of his silence, is a pseudonym with a lot to say: Kierkegaard very nearly named him as the author of *On the Point of View of my Work as an Author* (PV, 37)—what an astonishing stroke that would have been, for Kierkegaard to tell the story of his authorship in a voice that says it does not speak!

---

[1] Cf. Pattison's distinction between the pseudonyms and the 'regular fictional character[s]' that Kierkegaard uses; he then elaborates: 'Therefore he [Assessor or Judge William, as a "fictional character"] is far from being simply a mouthpiece for Kierkegaard's own views. At the same time, he presents ideas that anticipate or parallel those of other pseudonyms…' In what follows, I will treat both the characters and the pseudonyms as the expression of distinct perspectives, all of whom are dialectically engaged (2005: 91).

Johannes's silence indicates much: here an ostension, there a lacuna; in what is to come we will pay rapt attention to his varieties of silence. For now, we will begin with the general observation that his silence contains a profound—and, paradoxically, of course, an exceedingly loud—account of the human self as realized in faith.

Johannes de silentio's meditation focuses on the anticipatory Christian paradigm[2] of the faithful life, Abraham. Three features of this life are immediately apparent. First, a person who has faith acknowledges its ineluctable demands. Abraham has a necessary task, one that is uniquely his own: ' . . . take Isaac your only son, whom you love, go to the land of Moriah and offer him there as a burnt offering upon a mountain that I will show you.'[3] This task is not notional, but horrifyingly actual: Abraham must get up, saddle his donkey, prepare his servants and Isaac; he must cut the wood for the burnt offering. Abraham must travel three days, all the while mindful (in some sense) of the dreadful task—the absolutely necessary task—that he is undertaking.

Yes, but what *is* in Abraham's mind as he lives out, and bears out, this faithful assignment? Johannes of silence admits that thinking about Abraham's life presents a kind of conceptual impossibility: ' . . . when I must think about Abraham, I am virtually annihilated . . . At every moment I am aware of that prodigious paradox which is the content of Abraham's life . . . my thought cannot penetrate it . . . ' (FT, 27). This, of course, is the second distinctive feature of faith, that it is opaque. Abraham's task, for all of its necessity, is absolutely beyond reckoning; anyone who attempts to explain what Abraham is doing, or what Abraham takes himself to be doing, has instantly distorted and diminished the deed:

> [Abraham] believed that God would not demand Isaac of him, while he still was willing to sacrifice him if it was demanded. He believed by virtue of the absurd, for human calculation was out of the question, and it was indeed absurd that God, who demanded it of him, in the next instant would revoke the demand . . . Let us go further. We let Isaac

[2] More will be said about the ways in which Abraham, as rendered in *Fear and Trembling*, illuminates the phenomenon of Christian faith in the 'Fourth Movement' and 'Postlude'.

[3] Genesis 22:1–2.

actually be sacrificed. Abraham believed. He did not believe that he
would be blessed one day in the hereafter but that he would become
blissfully happy here in the world. God could give him a new Isaac, call
the sacrificed one back to life. He believed by virtue of the absurd, for
all human calculation had long since ceased. (FT, 29–30, emphasis mine)

Abraham cannot be understood: by Sarah, by Isaac, or even by
himself.

Faith's incomprehensibility, however, is preceded by a necessary
final reckoning, one that *does* demand utter clarity and coherence:
'Infinite resignation is the last stage before faith, so that whoever has
not made this movement does not have faith' (FT, 39). Johannes's
explanation of 'infinite resignation' suggests both a 'resigning from'
and a 'resigning to'; that is, a person must review life's lineaments, its
possibilities and limits, and become conceptually at home with them.
And what does that mean? It means, of course, that we human beings
are called to make an intellectual truce with the impossibility of our
undertakings: everyone we love and care for will die; the political
causes we champion will fade and be forgotten; the books we write,
the buildings we build—all of it is a vast and passing scene. To invest
ourselves in this finite, temporal life, to attempt to express the infinite
and the eternal within the bounds of the mortal, is folly. 'Resignation'
indicates that a person has the conceptual acumen to see this truth,
and understands that this temporal, corporeal situation is nothing in
relation to God's timelessness; this—as Johannes dubs him—'knight
of resignation' abandons any notion of achieving anything of ultimate
worth in this vale of tears.

Johannes elaborates on this theme by telling us a love story: 'A
youth falls in love with a princess and the whole content of his life
consists in this love, and yet the relation is such that it cannot possibly
be realized, cannot possibly be translated from ideality to reality' (FT,
34–5). The youth realizes that the finite is not a fit place for infinite
devotion: so what does he do? He translates his relationship into a
conceptual one; the *thought* of the princess is one that will not waver or
tarnish with the years:

> The love for that princess became for him the expression of an eternal
> love, assumed a religious character ... He keeps this love young, and it
> increases along with him in age and beauty. However, he needs no

finite occasion for its growth. *From the moment he has made the movement the princess is lost.* He does not need those erotic palpitations of the nerves from seeing the beloved etc., nor in a finite sense does he constantly need to take leave of her, because he recollects her in an eternal sense ... (FT, 36–7, emphasis mine)

In order to honor his infinite devotion, the youth resigns his actual, enfleshed, beloved to a specter of recollection. Note that this resignation is *infinite*; that is, a resigned person absolutely acknowledges the demands and limits of time and finitude. And so too for Abraham: a dead Isaac cannot be revived; the sacrifice of Abraham's cherished son would indeed be the irretrievable betrayal of a promise made to generations to come.

Faith, however, is able to 'move beyond'[4] the boundaries of resignation. Johannes de silentio finishes his story of the love-struck youth by introducing another knight: 'We shall now let the knight of faith appear in the incident previously mentioned. He does exactly the same as the other knight, he infinitely renounces the love that is the content of his life ... But then the miracle occurs ... he says: "I nevertheless believe that I shall get her, namely by virtue of the absurd, by virtue of the fact that for God everything is possible"' (FT, 39). Of course, the princess is still just as unobtainable: 'The understanding continued to be right in maintaining that in the world of finitude where it rules it was and remained an impossibility.' The knight of faith has resigned his love, but he claims that he will get her back again by virtue of the absurd: meaning, of course, he believes something that does not make any sense.

So: to return to Johannes's thoughts about Abraham, the 'Father of faith': Abraham's silence is therefore not a species of reticence (as if his words would be too fearsome for an ordinary listener). Abraham cannot say anything because there are no propositions, none, that can express the absurdity of his existential condition. The closest we can come to understanding what it is that Abraham believes, says Johannes, is that he believes that he can both have, and sacrifice, his Isaac, that a sacrifice will not entail the loss of Isaac: 'with God, all things are possible.'

---

[4] More about the trope of 'movement' momentarily.

Johannes de silentio also wants us to notice that faith[5] is utterly different from the conventional, calculating notion of hope: hope still lives within the margins of what is, and is not, humanly possible. Johannes imagines a young girl who has made a passionate wish: '. . . if in spite of all difficulties [she] is still convinced that her wish will be fulfilled, this conviction is not at all that of faith . . . her conviction dares not look the impossibility in the eye in the pain of resignation' (FT, 40). Johannes urges us to recognize that Abraham is not entertaining a mere *hope* that he may keep his cherished Isaac: his faith that he will keep him is an entirely different matter.[6] Here the silence of the incomprehensible begins.

But faith's silent opacity (when we tear ourselves away from this gripping, paradoxical scene) is also instructive. Abraham's faith cannot be understood because it is not a thought, or a belief, but *a way of being in the world*. When Abraham says 'Here I am', he is telling us that he is who he is as he does what he must (and, of course, what he must do—sacrifice Isaac, the sum and substance of his life—is precisely what cannot be done). Abraham's faith is in this sense immediate: it is actualized at every moment, from saddling up the donkey to preparing the sacrificial wood. This faith is not simply some *thought* about God's greatness,[7] or Isaac's infinite preciousness; rather, it is constituted by Abraham's deeds in the world, deeds that can only be thought about in what Johannes de silentio aptly calls a 'dialectical lyric' (FT, 1), a rhythmic, deft movement between an account of what faith is not, and an unspoken suggestion of faith's impossible contours.

So: faith is ineluctable, opaque, and realized at every moment by a way of being in the world: this is what Johannes de silentio means when he remarks, 'Temporality, finitude is what it is all

---

[5] In Danish, *'Tro'* means both 'faith' and 'belief'; de silentio's example of the girl's naïve certainty about getting her wish helps us to frame an important issue for this book: what is it that the faithful person 'believes'?

[6] The difference between ordinary 'hope', an attitude invested in a particular outcome, and the phenomenon of 'faith' is just one of the many distinctions we will have occasion to explore (and indeed is a central part of the phenomenological dimension of this account).

[7] We will have much more to say about the propositional content of faithful belief in the Fourth Movement and the Postlude.

about' (FT, 42)—Abraham's finite circumstance, as realized in time, is the site of his faith.

But the spectacle of Abraham's paradoxical condition dazzles; as Johannes de silentio reminds us, 'Abraham I cannot understand; in a certain sense I can learn nothing from him except to be amazed' (FT, 31). The paradoxical contours of Abraham's faithful existence are visible, but the interior of that life is impossible to apprehend. Johannes's inability to make sense of Abraham certainly informs his own— and very different—kind of silence: Johannes reminds us that he knows that 'God is love' but that he himself does not have the joy of faith (FT, 28). He can articulate the puzzle of faith, he can tell us what it is not and what it cannot be, but he, Johannes, does not *know* what it is to dwell in faith, and so he must refrain from speaking about his own experience of it.

—And here I too have been silent. In occupying ourselves with Johannes's account of Abraham, we have neglected the real object of my fascination, one of Johannes's own fictional creations. This character is also silent; Johannes depicts his actions in dumbshow, and yet his existence is meant to speak to us about what Johannes claims is the crucial element, the absolute source and centerpiece of human life: faith. Johannes de silentio admits that he has never met a 'knight of faith', but that he can readily imagine what this person is like.

Let's have a look at him:

> ... those who carry the treasure of faith easily deceive because their external appearance has a striking resemblance to that which both infinite resignation and faith deeply disdain—to bourgeois philistinism. I candidly admit that in my experience I have not found any authentic exemplar ... Nevertheless, I have sought in vain for several years to track one down. People generally travel around the world to see rivers and mountains, new stars, flamboyant birds, freakish fish, ludicrous breeds of humanity ... This does not occupy me. However, if I knew where such a knight of faith lived, I would travel on foot to him, for this miracle concerns me absolutely. I would not leave him for an instant but every minute pay attention to how he went about making the movements. I would consider myself settled for life and divide my time between watching him and practicing the maneuvers myself, and thus spend all my time admiring him. As I said, I have not found such a person; nevertheless, I can very well imagine him. Here he is.

> The acquaintance is made, I am introduced to him. The moment I first
> set eyes on him, that very instant I thrust him away from me, jump
> back, clap my hands together, and say half-aloud: 'Dear me! Is this the
> person, is it actually him? He looks just like a tax collector.' (FT, 32)

It is curious that Johannes de silentio's imagined knight of faith
resembles a keeper of that most detested of offices, someone who
collects taxes. A number of New Testament textual affinities and
clues tumble out: we are reminded of the apostle Matthew, who had
been a tax collector before becoming a follower of Jesus; Luke's story
of the tax man Zacchaeus, climbing the sycamore fig to get a better look
at Jesus (and then, after being caught out, suddenly becoming his dinner
host); the tax collector and the Pharisee, also from the Gospel of Luke (we
will get a better look at him in the 'Fourth Movement'). In short, there is a
cost to the life of faith, and it is—evidently—hardly pleasant to pay it.[8]

Setting aside these considerations of cost, debt, and paying what
one owes, let us continue to look at the figure Johannes de silentio has
conjured for us:

> ... I examine his figure from head to foot to see if there might not be a
> crack through which the infinite peeped out. No! He is solid through
> and through. His footing? It is sturdy, belonging entirely to finitude ...
> He enjoys and takes part in everything, and whenever one sees him
> participating in something particular, it is carried out with a persistence
> that characterizes the worldly person whose heart is attached to such
> things. He goes about his work. To see him one would think he was a
> pen-pusher who had lost his soul in Italian bookkeeping, so exact is he.
> He takes a holiday on Sundays. He goes to church. No heavenly look or

---

[8] The entire text of *Fear and Trembling* makes use of an economic metaphor:
Johannes de silentio begins with the observation that 'Not only in the commercial
world but in the realm of ideas as well, our age is holding a veritable clearance
sale ... ' (FT, 3); the set of 'Problems' set forth in *Fear and Trembling* begins with the
observation that 'An old adage drawn from the external and visible world says:
"Only the one who works gets bread ... In the world of the spirit ... it holds true
that only the one who works gets the bread, only the one who was in anxiety finds
rest ... "' (FT, 21); the Epilogue begins with this remark: 'On one occasion when
the price of spices in Holland became somewhat slack, the merchants let a few
loads be dumped at sea in order to drive up the price ... Do we need something
similar in the world of the spirit?' (FT, 107). We will have more to say about
Kierkegaard's 'economy' in what follows.

any sign of the incommensurable betrays him . . . his hearty, vigorous hymn-singing proves that he has a good pair of lungs. In the afternoon he takes a walk in the woods. He enjoys everything he sees, the throngs of people, the new omnibuses, the Sound . . . On the way he thinks about an appetizing little dish of warm food his wife surely has for him when he comes home, for example a roast head of lamb with vegetables . . . he does not have four beans, and yet he firmly believes that his wife has that delectable dish for him. If she has it, to see him eat would be an enviable sight . . . for his appetite is heartier than Esau's. If his wife doesn't have it—oddly enough, it is all the same to him. On the way he goes past a building site and meets another man. They talk a moment together; in no time he erects a building, having at his disposal all the resources required for that purpose. The stranger leaves him thinking he was surely a capitalist, while my admired knight thinks: 'Well, if it came to that I could easily get it.' He lounges by an open window and surveys the square where he lives. Everything that happens—a rat scurrying under a gutter plank, children playing— *everything engages him with a composure in existence* as if he were a girl of sixteen . . . absolutely to express the sublime in the pedestrian—that only the knight of faith can do—and that is the only miracle. (FT, 32–4, emphasis mine)

This portrait stands in comical juxtaposition to the awesome mystery of Abraham. Johannes de silentio, and indeed his readers, can barely stand to glance at the terrible, majestic equanimity of Abraham, his calm refrain of 'Here I am' always securely locating him in space and time as he proceeds with his impossible, necessary, and unthinkable (in both senses) task. The tax collector, this seeming 'bourgeois philistine' (de silentio's own comparison), is, on the other hand, entirely familiar (FT, 32).[9] This faithful fellow sings loudly in church, enjoys his work and his walks around Copenhagen; he takes pleasure in thinking about his supper.

What is so loveable—to me, at any rate—about this affable, humble character?

Let us take his measure for the moment.

My fascination with Johannes's faithful tax collector (I will now, and throughout, refer to him as 'the tax collector': yes, he only *looks* like

---

[9] Robert Perkins has aptly described the tax collector as 'a "gabber", a "hale fellow well-met"' (2007: 10).

one, and we will discover that how he appears and how he *is* are matters we ultimately need to consider)[10] is, properly speaking, a phenomenological one; that is, I am entranced by his mastery of simply being human. I am drawn to the way in which he is *located*.

Yes, *located.* The tax collector is supremely present—to himself, and to de silentio's audience—in a number of ways.

The tax collector is located in place. He is utterly absorbed by his surroundings, not plagued by the usual drift and distraction from which most of us suffer. Our tax collector easily and capably immerses himself in the very ordinary objects and events of his life without worry for them or distraction from the activity at hand. He focuses with precision on his work; he sings vigorously in church. He watches children play and rats scattering with what de silentio wonderfully calls a 'composure in existence'.

This supremely attentive and appreciative comportment is reminiscent of another, later nineteenth-century model of the highest life, the child described by Nietzsche in 'The Three Metamorphoses'. Here is Zarathustra's paean:

> I name you three metamorphoses of the spirit: how the spirit shall become a camel, and the camel a lion, and the lion at last a child ... what can the child do that even the lion cannot? Why must the preying lion still become a child? The child is innocence and forgetfulness, a new beginning, a sport, a self-propelling wheel, a first motion, a sacred Yes. Yes, a sacred yes is needed, my brothers, for the sport of creation: the spirit now wills its own will, the spirit sundered from the world now wins its own world.[11]

---

[10] It is worth noting that de silentio's character sketch is of a 'tax collector' rather than, as he is sometimes referred to in English-language scholarship, a 'shopkeeper': de silentio's exclamation of recognition is 'Herre Gud! er det Mennesket, er det virkeligt ham, han seer jo ud som en Rodemester.' The Danish noun 'Rodemester' usually means 'tax collector', or 'a citizen who is appointed to inspect certain public undertakings, especially as a tax collector, in one of the districts or quarters of a city (especially Copenhagen)' (*Molbech's Dictionary*, 1859). In the Fourth Movement, I will argue that the New Testament allusions invoked by this remark are crucial for interpreting Kierkegaard's intent across the many voices of his authorship.

[11] Nietzsche (1961: 54).

Zarathustra describes a hierarchy of spiritual development, one in which the highest form of life displays the marvelous self-absorption of a child, utterly at one with its activity. Our tax collector also 'wins his own world': he moves confidently about his environment, always finding himself meaningfully placed in the world, always already invested in the task at hand.[12]

He also, of course (and this thought is made fairly obvious by the locutions I've just used), anticipates one of Nietzsche's heirs, Heidegger, and his account of 'Being-in-the-world'. Heidegger, in *Being and Time*, radically retells the tale of what it is *to be*, and (more fundamentally) what it is to be a human being. Traditional philosophical accounts of the human condition typically describe a subject or rational agent moving through an objective environment; Heidegger argues that 'human being' is distinctively socialized into habits and practices which are only latterly rendered as 'concepts' or 'representations';[13] these propositional elements are not the source of our ability to navigate the world, but are in fact the theoretical detritus of how it is that humans actually dwell in a pre-reflectively meaningful domain. The world is thus always already available and meaningful to *Dasein* (human being), not in a thematically explicit way, but as a place of engaged action (just as Kierkegaard's aesthete finds his environment a terrain of possible enjoyment, haunted by the specter of boredom; more of this in the Second Movement).

Heidegger's *Dasein*, that 'being whose being is an issue for it',[14] is primordially understood as non-reflectively coping with tools and situations that are inherently meaningful. *Dasein* 'is what it does'; so too, in a sense, is our tax collector (that is, the tax collector seems to celebrate his human lot in *how* he does what he does). Indeed, Heidegger's rethinking of the nature of 'being' is deeply indebted to both Nietzsche and Kierkegaard; as Hubert Dreyfus puts it, 'Following Kierkegaard, [Heidegger] holds that Descartes's famous starting

---

[12] For more on Nietzsche's 'Three Metamorphoses', see Sheridan Hough (1997: 40–1).

[13] 'Being-in-the-world...amounts to a nonthematic circumspective absorption ...constitutive for the availableness of an equipmental whole...In this familiarity Dasein can lose itself in what it encounters in the world' Heidegger (1962: 107).

[14] Heidegger (1962: 32).

point should be reversed, becoming '"I *am*, therefore I think."'[15] The
contours of how it is that a person *is* in Kierkegaard's ontology is one
of the central concerns of this book. Of course, what Heidegger has
borrowed from Kierkegaard's work, and what he has made of these
polyphonic texts, is of considerable interest; in what follows, I will only
be concerned with recording those moments when Heidegger has
clearly made use of Kierkegaard's work (and when, perhaps, his
own work might shed some light on what Kierkegaard is up to).
I will also help myself to the Heideggerian lexicon when it seems
appropriate: we will have occasion to consider the human coping
skills that allow us to be absorbed in a task, the non-reflective availability of a particular social environment, and indeed the debt every
human owes to the cultural setting from which she or he emerges:
Husserl would identify this 'debt' as *intersubjectivity*, or the co-constitutive nature of human being.[16] Heidegger is certainly steering away
from any notion of a discrete subject, and he thus offers us *Mitsein*, or
'co-being': the Coda will consider what the tax collector's demeanor
can tell us about the ways in which human beings 'co-constitute' one
another.

The tax collector is located in time. His lived practice of faith limns his
finite, ever-changing condition with significance; he takes joy in what
is made manifest to him in his immediate circumstances. Life, when
lived faithfully, is immediately abundant and satisfying: at least, this
promise is suggested by the tax collector's blissful perambulations
around Copenhagen—with each step finding, as Johannes de silentio
says, 'the sublime in the pedestrian'. This happy rambler is utterly
absorbed in his life at this moment—*from* moment to moment—while
still indulging in wishes for the future (that delectable stew), managing
his tasks with precision ('. . . to see him one would think he was a pen-
pusher who had lost his soul in Italian bookkeeping, so exact is he . . . '
(FT, 32–3)), yet never out of touch with the wonder of his own
immediate existence, strung between (to borrow the words of another
pseudonym we will hear from shortly, Anti-Climacus) the finite and
the infinite, the temporal and the eternal, the necessary and the

[15] Dreyfus (1991: 3).
[16] Husserl's views on intersubjectivity were developed over many years: see
Husserl (1989, 1977, 1970).

possible (SUD, 13): strung between, but always securely expressing himself in the unfolding existential moment. This picture of a life fully realized right now—despite the absolute limits and inevitable regrets of the past, as well as the invitations and fearful taunts of an imaginary future—both fascinates and compels: 'He lets things take their course with a freedom from care as if he were a reckless good-for-nothing and yet buys every moment he lives at the opportune time for the dearest price, for he does not do even the slightest thing except by virtue of the absurd' (FT, 33–4). He is located in the present, the infinitely contentful present.

The tax collector is located in movement. He strolls the streets of Copenhagen, sings with gusto, eats with passion—indeed, the tax collector's appetite is said to be heartier than Isaac's own son Esau, who traded his birthright to his brother Jacob for a bowl of lentils. Esau, in relinquishing his inheritance, was no doubt mortally hungry, but the reader of Genesis can hardly imagine him taking much joy in his desperate meal.

'Movement' is Johannes de silentio's consistent image for the life of faith: 'I wonder', he muses, 'is anyone in my age actually capable of making the movements of faith?' (FT, 28). Such a 'movement', made by virtue of the absurd, allows a person 'to gain it [the finite] entire' (FT, 31). These movements can be described, but no one should mistake the description for the doing; Johannes remarks:

> If one wants to learn how to swim, one can let oneself be suspended in a sling from the ceiling and very well go through the motions, but one is not swimming. Likewise, I can describe the movements of faith, but...I make different movements. I make the movements of infinity, whereas faith does the opposite; after having made the movements of infinity, it makes those of finitude. (FT, 31)

Johannes, in searching for a knight of faith, tells us that he sizes up his candidates by looking 'only for the movements': such a person, as we have seen, moves through the world in a distinctive way. Johannes likens the tax collector's confident motion through life to *dancing*:

> [The knight of faith] resigned everything infinitely and then grasped everything again by virtue of the absurd. He constantly makes the movements of infinity, but he does it with such precision and proficiency that he constantly gets finitude out of it and at no second does

> one suspect anything else. It is supposed to be the most difficult task for
> a dancer to leap into a particular posture in such a way that there is no
> second when he grasps at the position but assumes it in the leap itself.
> Perhaps no dancer can do it—but this knight does. (FT, 34)

Johannes characterizes faith as embodying the poise, precision and
focus of a dancer, a dancer who is—impossibly—able to leap and,
proleptically, to be present in the next pose, all at once. (Here being
present in 'movement' seems to line up quite neatly with the way in
which the tax collector is located in time, with both future and past
being somehow fully realized in the present moment.)[17] We will
reconsider just what it means for our tax collector to dance in the
(In)conclusive Postlude.

And, most importantly: *the tax collector is located in pleasure.* Johannes
has occasion to remark, again and again, how the tax collector
continually takes joy in all things: 'he enjoys everything he sees, the
throngs of people, the new omnibuses, the Sound—to meet him on
the beach road one would think he was a mercenary soul taking a
break just to enjoy himself in this way...' (FT, 33): but he is not
'taking a break', because the pleasure he finds is comprehensive and
ongoing. Think of it: the tax collector enjoys (and, as Johannes
reminds us, takes part in) *everything*. It is this life of uninterrupted
pleasure that another of Kierkegaard's voices, A, passionately desires.
Of course, A's efforts to live a life wholly devoted to his own gratification (in all its variegated splendor) come to spectacular ruin. How,
then, does our tax collector do it? He achieves, with maddening,
enigmatic cheer, the unobtainable objective with which the Kierkegaardian quest sets sail.

One final thought about the tax collector's perpetual, contented
joy: his variety of (wholly quotidian) occupations—walking, singing,
strolling, rat-watching—do not seem to operate as 'pleasure-devices',
that is, as pursuits designed to elicit pleasure, but as *intrinsically* pleasing
activities, in that they reveal their meaningfulness *as* they are pursued.
(Again, this observation is reminiscent of the dancer who attains the

---

[17] Cf. Husserl's conception of phenomenological time, in which 'retentions' of
what has just been perceived conjoin with both impressions of what is immediately
perceived and 'protentions', anticipations of what will be perceived (1991).

next posture even before its execution: the tax collector becomes who he is as he takes up his faithful tasks, and the pleasure therein is just the pleasure of so living.) We will certainly think at greater length about the nature of pleasure and the life of faith in the Second Movement.

So: there he is, my well-loved and utterly mysterious tax collector. I find myself muttering a version of Johannes's own thought: 'yes, I could fly into a rage over it, if for no other reason than out of envy ...' (FT, 34). How does he do it? How is he able to be so (seemingly) carefree in the world, even with its disappointments, disasters, and ultimately the failure of those worldly projects?

Enough admiration. What follows are four explorations of the internal workings of this beautiful, enigmatic life. In honor of the relevant trope, I will call these essays 'movements', or turns on the Kierkegaardian dance floor. The pattern that emerges from these exertions really depends upon how faithful I remain to de silentio's alluring character sketch. And just how far *can* his delightful portrait take us? That is the question I am setting out to answer.

2

First Movement

The Aduton *of Selfhood*

> 'An author certainly must have his private personality as every-
> one else has, but this must be his *aduton* [sanctuary], and just as
> the entrance to a house is barred by stationing two soldiers with
> crossed bayonets, so by means of the dialectical cross of quali-
> tative opposites the equality of ideality forms the barrier that
> prevents all access.' (TA, 99)

Reflection and the Present Age

The faithful tax collector is clearly a self. Only selves can dwell in faith;
in fact, faith can be understood as the very functioning of the self as
she or he moves through the world: as Anti-Climacus remarks, 'Faith
is: that the self in being itself and in willing to be itself rests transparently in God' (SUD, 82).

What, then, *is* a 'self'? In his review of a novel, *Two Ages*,[1]
Kierkegaard—here speaking in his own voice—suggests that a self is
something far greater than merely being human. But the task of
becoming a self, Kierkegaard argues, has become nearly impossible for
the denizens of this present, passionless and indeed, as Kierkegaard
puts it, 'leveled' age: '...a reflective, apathetic age...stifles and
impedes, it levels. Leveling is a quiet, mathematical, abstract enterprise that avoids all agitation...leveling is an abstract power and is
abstraction's victory over individuals' (TA, 84).

---

[1] *Two Ages* is a review of Thomasine Gyllembourg's novel of the same name;
many English-speaking readers of Kierkegaard first encountered a portion of the
essay in a translation by Alexander Dru (1962).

The trope is apt: just as a bulldozer scrapes away the characteristic ruts and hillocks in a piece of land, so some (not yet identified) force has leveled the defining evaluative features of nineteenth-century Denmark's prevailing culture,[2] destroying what Kierkegaard calls 'the qualitative expression of difference between opposites'[3] (TA, 78). A 'qualitative distinction' is just that, an absolute difference in value between choices, and the disparity between the behaviors or the states of affairs that those value-driven choices ultimately produce. Take, for example, the case of going to school in the present age: 'This is not an insubordinate adolescent who still quivers and quakes before his schoolmaster. No, the relation is rather a certain uniformity in mutual exchange between teacher and pupil on how a good school should be run. Going to school means . . . being more or less interested in the problem of education' (TA, 79). The relationship of the teacher and the student is leveled because the qualitative difference between the teacher's knowledge and the student's ignorance no longer exists: it is no longer of any consequence that the teacher knows the difference between important material and passing trash because the structure of the teacher's own evaluation—the reasons why some books are worth reading and other are not—has been plowed over.

How do these evaluative structures get 'bulldozed'? Kierkegaard is clear that the central element in the process of cultural leveling is a kind of reflective enterprise. Reflecting, Kierkegaard argues, simply for reflection's sake, does not produce values, commitments or loyalties: like a House of Mirrors,[4] it only creates a dizzying spill of images, all seen in an infinite series of deferrals: 'Reflection's envy holds the will and energy in a kind of captivity. The individual must first of all break out of the prison in which his own reflection holds him, and if he

---

[2] Bruce Kirmmse (1990) provides a masterful account of Kierkegaard's Denmark, and the complacent Hegelianism of the intellectual elite.

[3] Dru's translation offers a more compressed version of 'qualitative disjunction of the qualities' as 'qualitative distinctions' (1962: 43).

[4] The pun is intended, and exists in the Danish (cf. the Hongs' introductory comments to their translation of *Two Ages*: '[Kierkegaard] also found his own multiple use of the word *reflection*, at times meaning the reflected image and effect of the age in private, domestic, and social-political life (Danish *Reflex*), and also reflection as deliberation (Danish *Reflexion*)' (TA, ix).

succeeds, he still does not stand in the open but in the vast penitentiary built by the reflection of his associates . . . ' (TA, 81).

But this claim is a curious one: why is it that simply reflecting on what we value, and thus act upon, and *why* we so value and so act, would flatten out the fundamental differences between what we value and what we do not? Of course, the 'reflective activity' in question here is familiar enough to us in our own media-saturated age: what Kierkegaard calls the 'prison' of reflection is nothing more than the infinite availability of yet another point of view, opinion, or aspect of the notion at hand. Consider the endless Web-parade of images and opinions, its torrential, quenchless, and indeed senseless variety: a person surfing the Internet to find an answer to a question or a definition of a term must be prepared to enter this very funhouse of reflection that Kierkegaard so aptly describes.

Back to our avid pupil: the teacher tells her that reading *Pride and Prejudice* is a worthwhile enterprise—but wait! This student has seen an advertisement for *Pride and Prejudice and Zombies*—why not read that version? After all, the book is based on Jane Austen's original, so perhaps this rendition constitutes a better read, since it also attends to the value of horror-genre entertainment. And so the dialectic of reflection continues, since neither the teacher nor the student can stake an absolute claim: another view, another reflective angle, is always possible:

> . . . beyond a doubt there is no task and effort more difficult for the individual as well as for the whole generation than to extricate oneself from the temptations of reflection, simply because they are so dialectical, because one single clever fabrication is able at any moment to reinterpret and allow one to escape somewhere, because even in the final moment of reflective decision it is possible to do it all over again . . . (TA, 77)

Is the teacher's assignment of Austen really a good one? Perhaps that's just her view, another book might be equally good, perhaps any book would be equally good, perhaps taking a nap would be just as good—and so on. *This* kind of reflective activity, says Kierkegaard, prevents us from taking a stand on our projects, and renders us incapable of absolutely committing ourselves to anything. When absolute (indeed, infinite) commitment—passion, as Kierkegaard reminds us—becomes impossible, then any activity is as good as the next. What can it matter what we do?

Of course, Kierkegaard is clear that explicitly thinking about our lives, even in a skeptical or comparative mode, is a good and necessary thing: ' . . . it must always be kept in mind that reflection itself is not something pernicious, that on the contrary the prerequisite for acting more intensively is the thorough kneading of reflection . . . ' (TA, 111). It is obvious that a person *needs* to reflect passionately on the values that give her projects their distinctive shape; an unreflective passion is surely worthless or even dangerous.[5] Here we are reminded of the difference between the knight of faith and the knight of resignation: the faithful knight has indeed accepted, become resigned to, the impossibility of realizing the infinite within the framework of finitude: and yet, having reflectively made his peace with the nature of things, he grasps faith by virtue of the absurd: 'The knight of faith . . . acknowledges the impossibility and at the same moment believes the absurd, for if he imagines himself to have faith without acknowledging the impossibility with all the passion of his soul and with his whole heart, then he deceives himself . . . since he has not even attained infinite resignation' (FT, 40). Johannes de silentio is clear that the faithful knight's passionate *reflection* on his mortal condition is necessary for the subsequent movement of faith.

What, then, is Kierkegaard's complaint? 'Reflection is not the evil, but the *state* of reflection, stagnation in reflection . . . ' (TA, 96, emphasis mine). The leveled condition of the present age's cultural terrain has made productive, edifying reflection nearly impossible; instead, Kierkegaard points out, the carefully considered claim has been replaced with a steady stream of chatter: 'When individuals are not turned inward in quiet contentment, in inner satisfaction, in religious sensitiveness, but *in a relation of reflection are oriented to externalities and to each other* . . . then chattering begins' (TA, 97–8, emphasis mine). And what is this talkativeness? 'It is the annulment of the passionate disjunction between being silent and speaking.' The destruction of this essential difference should be understood in terms of another leveled

---

[5] Kierkegaard seems to be reminding his readers, in true Socratic fashion, that the un-reflected-upon life is not worth living.

distinction, the difference between what is public and what is private: 'By this chattering the distinction between what is private and what is public is nullified in a private-public garrulousness, which is just about what the public is. For the public is public opinion that is interested in what is utterly private' (TA, 100).

Who, then, is this 'public'? 'The public is the actual master of leveling, for when there is approximate leveling, something is doing the leveling, but the public is a monstrous nonentity' (TA, 91).[6] The 'public' is a 'monstrous' abstraction, since the reflective condition (with its continually shifting focus) and leveling (which flattens the distinctions between contrastive elements) have emptied it of definitive content. Woe to anyone who hopes to have a significant life by aligning his views and attitudes with public opinion: 'If someone adopts the opinion of the public today and tomorrow is hissed and booed, he is hissed and booed by the public' (TA, 92). The 'public' is a 'phantom' who chatters about everything, and therefore talks about nothing in particular: 'chattering dreads the moment of silence, which would reveal its emptiness' (TA, 98).[7]

Kierkegaard condemns his own age as driven by the ceaseless murmur of public opinion, ever altering, never permitting an individual's convictions or private passions to stand.[8] How, then, to combat this inexorable process of de-valuation? We must, says Kierkegaard, acquire 'inwardness' by committing to a life project, one that uniquely identifies us as an individual: 'Character is inwardness... Reflection's envy holds the will and energy in a kind of captivity... this can be broken only by religious inwardness...' (TA, 78; 81).

---

[6] The notion of the public as a 'nonentity' stands to reason, since the voice of an individual would also necessarily be leveled.

[7] Heidegger's analysis of *Gerede*, 'idle talk', in Division I, section 5 of *Being and Time* makes ample use of Kierkegaard's own account of 'talkativeness' (1962); Kierkegaard's analysis of the 'Public' is certainly a resource for Heidegger's notion of *das Man.*

[8] Judge William (a voice we will meet in the Third Movement) has this to say about such persons: 'And this is sad when one contemplates human life, that so many live out their lives in quiet lostness; they outlive themselves... and vanish like shadows. Their immortal souls are blown away, and they are not disquieted by the question of its immortality, because they are already disintegrated before they die' (E/O, 2:168).

As we might expect, the 'inwardness' that constitutes the individual will not be available for public consumption. Consider: Abraham is a father, but his unique task is not to be understood as one among all the other instances of 'fatherhood'; so too for our tax collector, whose projects in the world are specific to him as he takes them up as his and his alone.

The public is a 'nothing': the individual, however, is made substantial by his passionate commitment to his life's project:

> ... a people, an assembly, a person can change in such a way that one may say: they are no longer the same; but the public can become the very opposite and is still the same—the public. But if the individual is not destroyed in the process, he will be educated ... to be satisfied in the highest religious sense with himself and his relationship to God, will be educated to make up his own mind instead of agreeing with the public, which annihilates all *the relative concretions of individuality*, to find rest within himself, at ease before God, instead of in counting and counting ... The aggregate is not the concretion that reinforces and educates the individual ... (TA, 92, emphasis mine)[9]

The individual's 'inwardness' gives him solidity of character: some things matter, others do not, and that 'mattering' is a private concern, one that is ultimately unavailable for public discourse. This, of course, is the very metaphor that Johannes uses to introduce our tax collector: 'I examine his figure from head to foot to see if there might not be a crack through which the infinite peeped out. No! He is solid through and through' (FT, 32).

An individual, made whole by a passionate commitment, is able to make the kinds of qualitative distinctions that the present age rejects: some subjects will be worth talking, and writing, and thinking about, and others will not, and the judgment about that relevance will take place in the *aduton* of selfhood, within the sanctuary created by that person's own commitment. This is why a talent for silence is a fundamental feature of the individual: 'Only the person who can

---

[9] Cf. Judge William's account of the self in *Either/Or* II: 'He chooses himself—not in the finite sense, for then this self would indeed be something finite that would fall among all the other finite things—but in the absolute sense, and yet he does choose himself and not someone else. This self that he chooses is infinitely concrete ... ' (E/O, 2:215).

remain essentially silent can speak essentially, can act essentially. Silence is inwardness' (TA, 97).[10] Perhaps one way of understanding the name of *Fear and Trembling*'s pseudonymous author—'Johannes of silence'—might be 'Johannes, who is devoted to the characteristic existential silence of the individual dwelling in faith.'

Selfhood

This notion of a substantial, individual self is a constant presence in Kierkegaard's thinking;[11] even in his last set of writings, a series of pamphlets called *The Moment,* Kierkegaard (here writing under his own name) describes the kind of person who is able to be in the right kind of love-relationship with God: '... the formula continues to be: the single individual in contrast to all the others' (TM, 188). But how does a person become such an individual? How is selfhood achieved?

In order to answer this question, we will take advice from another pseudonym, Anti-Climacus, the author of *The Sickness Unto Death* (1849) and *Practice in Christianity* (1850); Kierkegaard served as 'editor' for both volumes.

Why privilege the voice of Anti-Climacus? Anti-Climacus[12] writes as someone who has indeed established his own self through faith, and his exhortations and directives have the kind of (Christian) authority that Kierkegaard was unwilling to grant to himself. In his journals Kierkegaard reflects on creating this pseudonym: 'It is absolutely right—a pseudonym had to be used. When the demands of ideality

[10] Cf. Heidegger's remark about authentic discourse: 'Keeping silent authentically is possible only in genuine discoursing. To be able to keep silent, Dasein must have something to say—that is, it must have at its disposal an authentic and rich disclosedness of itself. In that case one's reticence [*Verschwiegenheit*] makes something manifest, and does away with "idle talk" [*Gerede*]' (1962: 208).

[11] Consider this paean from Kierkegaard: '... the movement is from the public to "the single individual." In other words, there is in a religious sense no public but only individuals... Oh, to what degree human beings would become—human and loveable beings—if they would become single individuals before God!' (PV, 10–11).

[12] The name 'Anti-Climacus' is clearly connected to another pseudonym, Johannes Climacus (cf. 'ladder'); 'anti' here indicates a 'coming before'. See the Historical Introduction to both *The Sickness Unto Death* and *Practice in Christianity*.

are to be presented at their maximum, then one must take extreme
care not to be confused with them himself, as if he himself were the
ideal' (SUD, xx).[13] By creating this pseudonym, Kierkegaard is able to
conduct an exploration of the human self as established in faith at a
remove; as he remarks in the posthumous *The Point of View on my Work
as an Author*, '... there appeared a new pseudonym, Anti-Climacus...
All the previous pseudonymity is lower than "the upbuilding author"
[i.e., Kierkegaard]; the new pseudonym is a higher pseudonymity'
(PV, 6).

So: here is what a supremely faithful Christian, the redoubtable
Anti-Climacus, has to say about becoming a self (in fact, this passage is
the book's opening salvo):

> A human being is spirit. But what is spirit? Spirit is the self. But what is
> the self? The self is a relation that relates itself to itself or is the relation's
> relating itself to itself in the relation; the self is not the relation but is the
> relation's relating itself to itself. A human being is a synthesis of the
> infinite and the finite, of the temporal and the eternal, of freedom and
> necessity, in short, a synthesis. *Considered in this way, a human being is still
> not a self.* (SUD, 13, emphasis mine)[14]

Human beings are born, but *selves* are created. A human being, Anti-
Climacus tells us, is a creature of opposed dimensions, a 'synthesis': of
infinity's endless reach and finitude's sink full of dishes, of eternal
truths and the creep of the hall clock, of the unbelievable—but
possible—outcome and the newsprint stamp of the given. Every
human must negotiate this divide, for every person is located in an
utterly specific historical, economic, cultural, and indeed bodily circumstance, all of which alters (or becomes more intransigent) over
time. But each person is also able to transcend these bare facts—one's
height and weight, class, religious upbringing (or lack thereof), habits,
and prejudices—by reconceiving her or his place in the scheme of
things. A human situation is given, but it can always become otherwise.

[13] Cf. Alastair Hannay's discussion of Kierkegaard's creation of Anti-Climacus
(2001: 374–5).

[14] The commentary on this passage, and, more generally, on Kierkegaard's
notion of the self, is vast. For two helpful elaborations on these passages, see John
D. Glenn Jr. (1987: 5–21), and Alastair Hannay (1987: 23–38).

This constitutional human tension, the opposition between a person's finite circumstance and the infinite possibilities for transformation, is everyone's birthright; a *self*, Anti-Climacus claims, is only established when a person 'takes a stand'[15] on this existential opposition. To achieve selfhood, a person must come to terms with these aspects of the human condition: 'If, however, the relation relates itself to itself, this relation is the positive third, and this is the self' (SUD, 13). But 'taking a stand' on the constitutional tensions of the human lot is not enough: a person must do so in the presence of God: 'in relating to itself and in willing to be itself, the self rests transparently in the power that established it' (SUD, 14). By relating to that which has established the whole relation—namely, by getting a determinate life-commitment in the presence of God—a person defines the factors that make up a human being. The 'infinite and finite' factors have to do with the nature of this self-relation, which is one of unconditional importance; this infinite worth is made manifest in specific, 'finite' choices. This infinitely significant self-relation demands specific kinds of recognition from the newly established self: by responding to the terms of her or his particular commitment, to its 'necessity', a person acquires an identity. Nonetheless, a person is ultimately free to decide how that commitment will be borne out in the world. Finally, the committed person must see the past, present, and future in terms of this undertaking; the 'temporal and the eternal' factors indicate that a person's commitment establishes continuity in life, even as that individual acknowledges the possibility of change.

Kierkegaard avers that a person's life commitment is not only established in the presence of God; this vocation, once embraced, is *itself* guided by a divine directive: Governance (*Styrelsen*). In *The Point of View*, Kierkegaard describes his own authorship as the product of Governance: 'It is Governance that has brought me up, and the upbringing is reflected in the writing process' (PV, 77). Kierkegaard points out that he certainly did not have an 'overview of the whole dialectical structure' in advance (PV, 76), but that every dialectical move now makes sense in terms of the entire project. (More of the puzzle of *Styrelsen* in the Postlude.)

---

[15] What it means to 'take a stand' will be discussed in the Second Movement.

This notion of comprehensive 'sense making' is of considerable interest. Again, Kierkegaard uses himself as an example of the way in which the quotidian accident may suddenly become fruitful or loom large in the scheme of things:

> It has been inexplicable to me how very often seemingly quite accidental little circumstances in my life, which then in turn admittedly became something very considerable through my imagination, brought me into a specific state, and I did not understand myself, became depressed—and see—then out of this developed a mood, *the very mood I should use in the work with which I was engaged at the time*, and at just the right place. (PV, 76, emphasis mine)

The work of writing always involves lapse and doubt and a self-reflexive survey of the project that is emerging, but those critical pauses (or ruptures, or moments of full-throated writerly despair) are *themselves* part of the shape and texture of the finished project.[16]

In one of his later discourses, Kierkegaard poses a series of questions to a self who has committed to a vocation, questions about how this individual understands her or his occupation and intimate relationships: does this person acknowledge '... that even in the relationships we human beings call the most intimate you recollect that you have an even more intimate relationship, the relationship in which you as a single individual relate yourself to yourself before God?' (UDVS, 129). Is this self, in living out its 'eternal purpose', properly oriented to fulfill the quotidian demands of this vocation (UDVS, 93)? '*In the course of your occupation, what is your frame of mind, how do you perform your work?* Are you convinced that your occupation is your calling so that you do not reinterpret it according to the results and think that it is not still your calling?' (UDVS, 139). An established self is meant to conduct his or her projects in relation to the life-commitment he or she has made, and to refrain from making judgments about the ongoing success (or failure) of the work at hand.

Here, perhaps, we might help ourselves to an ordinary notion of 'faith' (one that grafts on rather neatly to this picture of a self

---

[16] This dialectical observation is wholly Hegelian: cf. the plant from the Preface to the *Phenomenology of Spirit* wherein the blossom does not negate the bud, but is its passionate realization (1977).

that is actualized in faith): a self has confidence from moment to moment in a vocational outcome, because everything can be—and will be—made use of, no matter how ordinary or disruptive (or indeed catastrophic).

The Apostle James and 'Epistemic Flexibility'

—But having so described the 'confidence' of our faithful self, we can see that this is no ordinary thought at all. Far from it. In fact, we now arrive at the cherished, all-important New Testament touchstone of Kierkegaard's thinking, James 1:17–21.

Don't take my word for it. Here is what Kierkegaard has to say about James 1:17–21 in a journal entry from August, 1855: 'If a person were permitted to distinguish among biblical texts, I could call this text (James 1:17–21) my first love, to which one usually (*always*) returns at some time; and I could call this text my only love— to which one returns again and again and again and *always*' (TM, 602).

And here it is:

> Every good and every perfect gift is from above, and comes down from the Father of Lights, with whom there is no change or shadow of variation. According to his own counsel, he brought us forth by the word of truth, that we should be a first fruit of his creation. Therefore, my beloved brethren, let every man be quick to hear, slow to speak, slow to anger, because a man's anger does not work what is righteous before God. Therefore put away all filthiness and all remnants of wickedness and receive with meekness the word that is implanted in you and that is powerful for making your souls blessed.

This verse from James has a curious and important relation to our tax collector. One of Kierkegaard's discourses on this verse, titled 'Every Good and Every Perfect Gift', was published in May, 1843, five months before the release of *Fear and Trembling*; two more treatments of 'Every Good and Every Perfect Gift' were published seven weeks later. It turns out that Kierkegaard's author, Johannes de silentio, and his own creation, our tax collector, are both embedded—at least in

the temporal terms of Kierkegaard's authorship—in a longer meditation on this verse from the Apostle James.[17]

So: 'Every good gift and every perfect gift is from above and comes
down from the Father of lights, with whom there is no change or
shadow of variation.'—How are we meant to begin with this immediately (for me, anyway) *dis*comforting verse?

Kierkegaard makes it clear that this passage is a difficult one: 'These
words are so comprehensible, so simple, and yet how many were they
who really understood them, really understood that they were a
commemorative coin more magnificent than all the world's treasure,
but also a small coin that is usable in the daily affairs of life?'
(EUD, 39).[18] The difficulty of the verse is an epistemological one:
how does a person *know* when she has received one of God's good and
perfect gifts? How to distinguish one of *God's* gifts from the happy
accident, the piece of misfortune, or indeed the act of evil?

Human beings are, of course, unable to make these discriminations,
and their determination to achieve this kind of certainty is their
downfall: '"...is it possible for...[the] understanding to decide
with certainty what is a good and perfect gift for him? Does it not
run aground on this again and again?..." With that, doubt was all
through with its explanation of the words—and also all through with
the words. It had changed the apostolic, authoritative saying into
empty talk...' (EUD, 41). Instead, Kierkegaard reminds his reader
that the quest for this kind of certainty must be abandoned:

> ...this certitude...was denied you. But then, when the busy thoughts
> had worked themselves weary, when your fruitless wishes had exhausted
> your soul, perhaps then your being grew more calm, perhaps your mind
> ...developed in itself the meekness that is receptive to the word that was
> implanted in your soul, the word that all good and perfect gifts come
> from above. Then no doubt you confessed in all humility that God surely

[17] The connections between Kierkegaard's signed writings, both early and late,
and Anti-Climacus's robustly Christian account of the self, are of considerable
interest; for now we should attend to the (in)famous Heideggerian footnote in *Being
and Time*, reminding us that there is more to be learned from Kierkegaard's
'upbuilding' writings than from his theoretical ones (1962: 494).

[18] Again, Kierkegaard's familiar economic trope is at work; more about the use
of these metaphors as we proceed.

did not deceive you when he accepted your earthly wishes and foolish desires, exchanged them for you and instead gave you divine comfort and holy thoughts; that he did not treat you unfairly when he denied you a wish but in compensation created this faith in your heart, when instead of a wish, which, even if it would bring everything, at most was able to give you the whole world, *he gave you a faith by which you won God and overcame the whole world.* (EUD, 36, emphasis mine)

The 'holy thought', and indeed the content of faith's 'knowledge', is the claim that *every* gift is good and perfect: '...just as God's almighty hand made everything good, so he, the Father of lights, ever constant, at every moment makes everything good, makes everything a good and perfect gift for everyone who has enough heart to be humble...' (EUD, 41).[19]

What can it possibly mean to claim that at every moment 'everything is good'? If a person claims to 'know' that every gift is good and perfect, what manner of 'knowledge' is this?

In thinking about what it is that faith permits us to know, let us return to Johannes de silentio's homespun illustration, our faithful tax collector: what does this seemingly unremarkable philistine, drawn from the bourgeois ranks of Golden Age Denmark, *know* about his own life circumstances? Recall that as our tax collector travels home, he thinks that his wife will have prepared lamb's head stew for dinner: 'It so happens that he does not have four beans, and yet he firmly believes that his wife has that delectable dish for him... his wife does not have it—*curiously enough, he is just the same*' (FT, 33, emphasis mine).

What, then, did the tax collector *know* when he anticipated the stew?

Clearly, he did not know that he would have his favorite meal; rather, he was holding a false belief. Why, then, doesn't he respond with a fitting epistemic affect: surprise, irritation, disappointment? How can he be 'just the same'?

First, the knight's intentional state—whatever it is—must be distinguished from merely *wanting* or *hoping* for stew. To underscore this difference, recall de silentio's description of a young girl who '... in

---

[19] It is surely worth noting that 'everything' is a *gift*: no currency, actual or existential, is involved in this bestowal.

spite of all difficulties is still convinced that her wish will be fulfilled, [whose] conviction is not at all that of faith . . . ' (FT, 40). The girl can, and will, be frustrated when her wish is not granted: but the knight suffers no such disappointment. He is, to pun badly, always already 'appointed': if the knight gets the stew supper he loves, then he rejoices; if he gets bread and water, then *that* is the appointed meal, and thus an occasion to embrace.

What, then, is the content of the knight's belief? Regardless of its content—a question we will return to momentarily—that belief is held faithfully. Faith gives the knight what we might call a kind of 'epistemic flexibility'. The 'flexibility' that characterizes faith paradoxically under-stands the fixed, limited, and finite conditions of a person's life to be infinitely overflowing with possibilities for grace and goodness.

If every gift is a good and perfect one from God, then the tax collector, and indeed every faithful petitioner, must give thanks for all things: 'And when your allotted portion was sufferings, did you thank God? And when your wish was denied, did you thank God? And when you yourself had to deny your wish, did you thank God? And when people wronged and insulted you, did you thank God?' (EUD, 43). Kierkegaard hastens to remark that thanking God for evil suffered does not make it less *evil*: 'We are not saying that their wrong ceased to be wrong—what would be the use of such pernicious and foolish talk! It is up to you to decide whether it was wrong; but have you taken the wrong and insult to God and by your thanksgiving received it from his hand as a good and perfect gift? Did you do that?' (EUD, 43).

The issue is not the gift,[20] but God's infinite transformational power, a power that is made available by faith. God can make *any* gift good and perfect: so says faith.

---

[20] Heidegger, in one of his later works, also (in a Kierkegaardian mode) reminds his reader to think about the fundamental nature of a gift: 'When we give thanks, we give it for something. We give thanks for something by giving thanks to him whom we have to thank for it. The things for which we owe thanks are not things we have from ourselves . . . We receive many gifts, of many kinds. But the highest and really most lasting gift given to us is always our essential nature, with which we are gifted in such a way that we are what we are through it. That is why we owe thanks for this endowment, first and unceasingly' (1968: 142).

Here, then, is what the faithful tax collector 'knows': 'every gift is good and every gift is perfect'. A kiss or a kick, a bouquet or a bullet—all of it is good and perfect. This claim—alarming, I think, in its lapidary assurances about our lives—wreaks havoc with our usual notions of epistemic conditions of satisfaction. If the faithful tax collector believes that he will have stew for supper, then the only condition that can satisfy that belief is 'that the meal is lamb's head stew'; however, when the dinner is, say, bread and water, he is not disappointed: in fact, he is just the same. He is content; he is satisfied. This is because faith paradoxically sees the world's absolute limits as infinitely abundant and life-affirming. *Any* 'conditions' will satisfy *any* belief, any state of affairs will do: no state of affairs is beyond God's power, and the power to make all gifts good and perfect just *is* the activity of faith. As Kierkegaard remarks,

> You did not anxiously question what it is that comes from God; you happily and boldly said: This, for which I thank God. You did not trouble your mind with deliberating over what was a good and perfect gift, because you confidently said: I *know* that this for which I am thanking God is that, and therefore I thank him for it ... You did not insist on learning much from life; you wished to learn but one thing: always to thank God, and thereby to learn to understand one thing: that all things serve for good who love God. (EUD, 42, emphasis mine)

This approach decisively puts us out of reach of the most basic tenets of epistemology; however, it does shed some light on the nature of the *paradox* in question. To return to Johannes de silentio's remark about the thought that governs the knight of faith: 'I nevertheless believe ... by virtue of the absurd, by virtue of the fact that for God everything is possible' (FT, 39). With God, all things are possible because every harsh necessity paradoxically contains God's utter abundance.

A story told by one of my mentors, the late Paul Feyerabend, serves as a useful analogy for the epistemic flexibility of faith. In his autobiography, Feyerabend describes the moment when, during a battle on the Russian Front, he was felled by a bullet:

> Suddenly my face was burning. I touched my cheek. Blood. Next, an impact on my right hand. I looked at it. There was a large hole in my glove. I didn't like that at all. The gloves were made of excellent leather and lined with fur; I would have liked them to remain intact ...

I slipped and fell. I tried to get up but I couldn't. I felt no pain, but I was convinced that my legs had been shattered. For a moment I saw myself in a wheelchair, moving along endless shelves of books—I was almost happy... I soon recovered but remained paralyzed from the waist down. I was not unduly concerned... I didn't mind being a cripple— I was content; I talked to my neighbors; read novels, poems, crime stories, essays of all kinds.[21]

Feyerabend, in the moment of his grievous injury, was able to be 'almost happy' about his paralysis: he saw his wound as an opportunity to return to his studies, rather than the decisive end to his youthful vigor.—Of course, it *was* the decisive alteration and diminution of his physical powers: he would never again walk without crutches, or be free of persistent pain. And yet he did not see it so: while his intellect made the new limitations imposed on him all too clear, his 'epistemic flexibility' allowed him to take up 'limitation' as 'new life'.[22]

Let us press the story further. What is it that Feyerabend knows about his condition? Certainly, he has ordinary, conventional knowledge about the extent of his injuries; from these facts, he can draw some conclusions about the future: he will never again be able to walk without assistance; he will suffer chronic pain; he will be obliged to endure many hours of rehabilitative physical therapy. Because of damage to his spinal cord, he will be permanently impotent. Now let us imagine a 'Feyerabend the Faithful', a person who lives in the Christian faith of Religiousness B: what is it that he knows beyond these ordinary justified, true beliefs?

Feyerabend the Faithful knows that he is disabled and in pain, and that he can anticipate so remaining; he also 'knows' that this condition is a good and perfect gift. Of course, this 'knowledge' flies in the face of his ordinary knowing: surely disability and chronic suffering are neither good nor perfect. *But they can be taken up as such.* To repeat the words of Kierkegaard: '... I know that this for which I am thanking God is [a good and perfect gift]... ' (EUD, 42).

---

[21] Paul Feyerabend (1995: 52–4). It is perhaps noteworthy that Feyerabend mentions reading Kierkegaard during his recovery (1995: 58).

[22] Sartre's notion—borrowed from Bachelard—of the 'coefficient of adversity' is an utterly Kierkegaardian principle of this sort (1956: 428).

'Truth is Subjectivity'

What, then, does it mean to 'take up' that which is clearly painful as something that is good and perfect? Here we arrive at one of the central insights of Kierkegaard's authorship, the notion that 'truth is subjectivity'. This infamous slogan from the *Concluding Unscientific Post-script* is, as slogan-reduced notions often are, widely misunderstood;[23] as Robert Perkins rightly points out, it is more sensibly rendered as 'the truth is the subjectivity'.[24] Perkins continues: 'First, and most important, Kierkegaard does not destroy the distinction between truth and falsehood. Rather he reiterates this distinction by insisting that one can be subjectively in untruth as well as in the truth. One's commitment to X does not make X true.'[25] In fact, we misplace our attention if we focus on the truth, or untruth, of what our faithful person believes: the perspicuous phenomenon is instead the *development* of the subjective individual. Perkins concludes, 'An existing human being is in the process of becoming and so is his truth.'[26]

The 'process of becoming' is another name for the ongoing task of what Kierkegaard calls 'upbuilding'. In a more recent analysis of Kierkegaard's radical reshaping of traditional epistemology, Perkins explores this line of thinking:[27] 'Upbuilding suggests a certain view of the person. Upbuilding suggests that a person is unfinished, in process... Only if a person is unfinished is upbuilding possible; only if a person is unfinished can we speak of choice, options and freedom... As a person constitutes himself in an elaborate group of modalities he is built up... Upbuilding truths provoke us, elicit our commitments, form our lives.'[28]

Here we have a refinement of the notion of subjectivity: a subject is best understood not as a static entity, but as a dynamic development. A person's beliefs about the world, when examined subjectively, are properly evaluated, as Johannes Climacus puts it, in relation to that person's orientation to and understanding of the utterly local context

---

[23] Merold Westphal provides a useful catalogue of the ways in which this 'notorious suggestion' has been misinterpreted (1996: 114–33).

[24] Perkins (1973: 211). [25] Perkins (1973: 211).

[26] Perkins (1973: 212). [27] Perkins (1990: 8).

[28] Perkins (1990: 11).

in which these beliefs are borne out: 'When the question about truth is asked subjectively, reflection is directed subjectively to *the nature of the individual's relationship*; if only the mode of this relationship is in the truth, the individual is in the truth even if he should happen to be thus related to what is not true' (CUP, 1:199, emphasis mine).[29]

What does Johannes Climacus mean by 'the nature of the individual's relationship' (or indeed the 'mode' of the relationship)? Obviously, the *relationship* between the subject and what the subject is claiming is the crucial element here. In order to see what is actually at stake in this 'relational' claim, let us start with the best possible subject-utterance condition: a subject makes a truth claim, and the subject's utterance is in fact true. Surely here we have the right kind of relation, one that offers us an example of 'truth is subjectivity'?

Well, no: not necessarily. Oddly enough, a Socratic analogy will help us out here. Recall that in the *Meno*, Socrates makes the bold and rare assertion that he knows something: he knows the difference between *orthê doxa*, correct opinion, and *epistêmê*, knowledge (Plato, *Meno*, 98b). This claim is a response to Meno's remark that he cannot see any difference: a true belief that X and knowledge that X surely have identical content (*Meno*, 97d).

Meno is (in part) right: the difference between *orthê doxa* and *epistêmê* is not a matter of content. Two persons holding the same belief cannot be distinguished on the basis of, say, an utterance; both will claim 'X'. The difference between the two is *how* the belief is held. A true belief is less reliable: it is not located in a network of relevant justified true beliefs, and the beliefs to which it is attached are not relevant in the right way. Rote memorization can offer up a series of truths, but the person giving the recitation does not actually understand what it is that she or he is saying.[30] Knowledge, of course, is a true belief that

---

[29] Perkins concludes, 'Kierkegaard rehabilitates the individual, the ordinary walking down the street variety of human being. What is the concept of truth that would be pertinent to a person, simply as a person, a person in the process of becoming? Or better, how is the person related to what the person considers to be the truth?' (1990: 14).

[30] Meno gives a brilliant example of this at the beginning of the dialogue when Socrates quizzes him about the definition of 'virtue'. Each response, as the end of the dialogue bears out, has some truth to it, but not in the rote way that Meno has mastered his responses, nor in precisely the way he intended.

is held in the right way: it stands in the proper relation to other pieces of knowledge; it can be accounted for, and recognized when approached from any epistemic perspective. This gives knowledge the solidity and reliability that is its hallmark.

Now the issue is clear: merely holding, and espousing, a true belief is not necessarily to be in the right *relation* to that truth. Johannes Climacus provides a trenchant example of such a truth-claimant in the *Postscript*: he imagines a madman who has escaped from an asylum. Of course, the madman does not want to be captured and taken back: what to do? He realizes that he must convince everyone around him that he is in fact sane, and how better to do this than to speak the objective truth? Climacus continues:

> As he is walking and pondering this, he sees a skittle ball lying on the ground. He picks it up and puts it in the tail of his coat. At every step the ball bumps him... and every time it bumps him he says, 'Boom! The world is round.' He arrives in the capital city and immediately visits one of his friends. He wants to convince him that he is not lunatic and therefore paces up and down the floor and continually says, 'Boom! The world is round.' But is the earth not round? (CUP, 1:195)

And indeed the earth is: the fault of the madman's recitation does not lie in the truth of the utterance, but in his relation to it. His objectively true remark is subjectively empty; it functions as a kind of incantation to ward off the asylum supervisor, rather than as a meaningful remark about the world through which he moves.

'Truth is subjectivity' is thus, in part, a meditation on the way in which a truth is held. But what does this observation have to do with what Kierkegaard presents as the 'epistemic claim' made in James 1:17? As we have already seen, the 'epistemic flexibility' that this verse entails effectively rules out the usual conditions of satisfaction: any condition will satisfy any belief, because every 'gift', at every moment, is rendered as 'good and perfect'. Evidently, the faithful belief that 'Every gift is good and every gift is perfect' is the most fundamental expression of 'truth is subjectivity': the faithful subject becomes passionately engaged in the world as it is made manifest by that subject, from moment to moment.

Johannes Climacus makes it clear that this is a temporal resolution, one that illuminates a subject's finite circumstances. As he puts it: 'In the moment of the decision of passion, where the road swings off from objective knowledge, it looks as if the infinite decision were thereby finished. But at the same moment, the existing person is in the temporal realm, and the subjective "how" is transformed into a striving that is motivated and repeatedly refreshed by the decisive passion of the infinite, but it is nevertheless a striving' (CUP, 1:203). The tax collector once again strolls into view: there he is, at every moment wholly absorbed and invested in his surroundings, which continue to unfold as 'good and perfect' through his faithful striving (which is, as Climacus points out, 'repeatedly refreshed' by the truth that he subjectively holds).

To return to our imagined Feyerabend the Faithful: his 'subjective truth' has taken him away from his actual, objective condition. This 'subjective truth', that 'all gifts are good and perfect', does not undermine—or even acknowledge—his objective condition: the faithful Feyerabend certainly knows, and accepts, that he suffers, and will suffer; he knows that his body has been forever altered, its abilities circumscribed: and yet he subjectively 'knows' that his suffering will be the occasion for growth, and ultimately joy.

Recall the quotidian joy of our faithful tax collector: it is interesting to note two ways in which his manner of moving through the world completes the thought begun in the three *Upbuilding Discourses* on 'Every Good and Every Perfect Gift'. First, consider one of Kierkegaard's declarations about the words of the Apostle James: if understood properly, claims Kierkegaard, they are 'a commemorative coin more magnificent than all the world's treasure, but also a small coin that is usable in the daily affairs of life' (EUD, 39). This thought, says Kierkegaard, is a 'magnificent' one, and surely a theoretical palliative in confronting life's exigencies—but it is also meant to plunge us back into life in much the way that the faithful tax collector securely 'purchases' his world: ' . . . at every moment he lives at the opportune time for the dearest price, for he does not do even the slightest thing except by virtue of the absurd . . . he has felt the pain of renouncing everything . . . and yet the finite tastes just as good to him as to one who never knew anything higher, for his remaining in finitude has no trace of a dispirited, anxious training, and yet he has this *confidence* to delight in it as if it were the surest thing of all' (FT, 34, emphasis mine).

Evidently, our tax collector has mastered the art of paying with the 'small coin' of faith (a 'smallness' that is infinitely 'large').

The tax collector's faithful existence also amplifies and completes one of Kierkegaard's direct claims about what faith can achieve: faith will allow you to 'win God' and 'overcome the whole world'. The tax collector, however, is content simply to *dwell* in the world: its abundance is complete and absolute.

But these conclusions are too quick, too facile. The verse from James only serves as a place to begin, and the tax collector's kind of 'epistemic flexibility' needs to be located in the larger frame of Kierkegaard's project.[31] What about despair? What about sin, and suffering? Why does Kierkegaard, in one of his final pamphlets, tell us that '... what God wants—out of love—is that a person shall die to the world, that if God is so gracious as to turn his love toward him, that what God then does—out of love—is to torment him in all the agonies designed to take life away from him, because it is this that God wants ... he wants to have the life of the one who is born, wants him transformed into one who has died, someone who lives as one who is dead ... ' (TM, 251). What has become of our cheerfully fulfilled bourgeois philistine, dwelling in satisfied abundance? Is it simply the case that Kierkegaard's Christian polemics must ultimately blot out Johannes's happy existential portrait?

The interiority of the faithful life, as Kierkegaard and Anti-Climacus depict it, needs to be examined, and our tax collector will be held to account. For now, however, we will look more closely at the tax collector's most immediate and attractive feature, his mysterious, comprehensive cheer.

---

[31] Cf. the remarks of Johannes Climacus in the *Postscript* (CUP, 500).

3

Second Movement

Choosing Pleasure

'[He] is ideally intoxicated with himself... even the most multifarious pleasures of actuality are too little for him compared with
what he enjoys in himself.' (E/O, 1:134)

Ideal Intoxication

Ah, pleasure. Yes! I'll have some, please. Will you?

Our (literally) self-possessed tax collector certainly seems to be
having a good time: 'he enjoys and takes part in everything...' (FT,
32). What does our well-pleased tax collector suggest about the
relation of pleasure to the life of faith?

Perhaps the question itself seems odd: why would we assume that
faith has anything at all to do with being pleased? But indeed the
whole Kierkegaardian odyssey begins in the pursuit of pleasure. And it
is only after entering the aesthetic sphere or stage of life that a person
is even eligible for selfhood: in the aesthetic 'sphere', a person first
learns how to attempt a passionate commitment by focusing desire; it
is here that the ability to 'will one thing'[1] gets its start.

More needs to be said about these so-called 'spheres' or 'stages'. We
began with the observation that Kierkegaard 'entertains' a variety of
voices—that is to say, *not* the claim that Kierkegaard the author 'uses'
these voices. This distinction is important in understanding what a
'sphere' or 'stage of life' is. The 'use' of different characters and

---

[1] This is a central motif of *Upbuilding Discourses in Various Spirits*; more of this
theme in the Fourth Movement.

authors suggests that Kierkegaard, Puppet-Master, deploys his poly-
vocal cast with a final message firmly in mind, that he has in each case
manipulated a character's speech to achieve a comprehensive, imbri-
cated effect.[2] Far from it: as we have already seen, Kierkegaard denies
that his authorship was guided by his own plan for its final shape: only
in hindsight, Kierkegaard claims, is the total purpose and point of
these texts made manifest (PV, 77).

Kierkegaard's characters have a kind of integrity that a mere
illustration or stage prop necessarily lacks. As literary creations,
these voices speak from, and about, a world that they inhabit. The
conclusions we draw about how things are for them (and the significance of their way of life) are up to us: Kierkegaard's 'method' (if one
can call it that) is to let these characters speak for themselves. As
readers, we can listen carefully to each person, and understand that
his (or, on occasion, her) comments reveal a commitment to a particular way of life. It is a steadfast devotion to a particular life-pursuit
that informs their opinions and claims, and that locates a character in
a life 'stage' or 'sphere'.

Here is how Frater Taciturnus, the final authorial voice in *Stages on
Life's Way* (1845), describes the 'spheres':

> There are three existence-spheres: the esthetic, the ethical, the reli-
> gious. The metaphysical is abstraction, and there is no human being
> who exists metaphysically. The metaphysical, the ontological, is [*er*],
> but it does not exist [*er ikke til*], for when it exists it does so in the esthetic,
> in the ethical, in the religious... The ethical sphere is only a transition
> sphere, and therefore its highest expression is repentance as a negative
> action. The esthetic sphere is the sphere of immediacy, the ethical the
> sphere of requirement (and this requirement is so infinite that the
> individual always goes bankrupt), the religious the sphere of fulfillment,
> but, please note, not a fulfillment such as when one fills an alms box or
> a sack with gold, for repentance has specifically created a boundless
> space and as a consequence, the religious contradiction: simultaneously
> to be out on 70,000 fathoms of water and *yet be joyful*. (SLW, 476–7,
> emphasis mine)

[2] Roger Poole aptly describes the 'blunt reading' of Kierkegaard that renders
his multifarious texts as vehicles for Christian 'edifying' (*opbyggelige*) (1998: 58–66).

Frater Taciturnus's account here is rich with important details that we must return to later. For now, we can begin with the notion that these stages or spheres stake out (roughly) three different strategies for bringing together the synthetic aspects of being human. Anti-Climacus, in limning the nature of the human frame, reminds us that we are born into an ineluctable tension: the necessary demands of temporality and finitude must somehow accommodate the timelessness of the infinitely valuable. Of course, as Kierkegaard points out in *Two Ages*, most people never rise to the challenge of selfhood—they are simply pulled from one putative source of significance to the next. For most human beings, everything is (potentially) important, and, as a consequence of modernity's restless reflective condition, no pursuit, no discipline, can ever be established as absolutely more important than any other.

A self, as we saw in the First Movement, is created when a person faithfully takes up her or his unique vocation in the presence of God; that commitment provides focus for the competing demands of the human constitution. Using this formula, let us surmise what we can about our tax collector (knowing full well that this is as yet still a wholly external (and in that sense superficial) assessment). The tax collector must constantly express his infinite devotion to his life's work (and indeed the infinite worth he finds in his vocation) as he makes his way through a very ordinary, finite, landscape. Even though his surroundings change, his passion for his life's work does not: his humble, everyday activities—perambulating, singing, dreaming of stew—are given eternal significance by his infinite passion.

Our tax collector dwells in faith, meaning that he resolves the native synthetic tension of being human by living out the life-task that is uniquely his. There are, however, other (and ultimately unsatisfactory) ways of resolving the competing demands of being human: here is where the journey to selfhood—and to faith—begins.

When a human being enters into a sphere or stage of existence, he or she—beset with the endless yammer of popular opinion, unable to stake a claim about what really matters—suddenly achieves a provisional wholeness and personhood through this commitment to a way of life, a wholeness that removes a person from the 'leveling' processes of the public arena (E/O, 2:191). Famously, as Frater Taciturnus has already summed up for us (though this simplifies matters greatly),[3] there are three such kinds of life-commitments, the aesthetic, the ethical, and the religious. Just to get started, we will identify the first of these as the life of pleasure (to take the designation at its (Greek) word, *aisthetikos*, the root of which suggests a life devoted to feeling, sensation, and not primarily to do with art or artistic production) and, on the other hand, the life formed by deliberation and choice (again, the Greek *ethikos*, or 'character', helps us to understand what is at stake here).

We can state the issue in another, more provocative way: the expression 'stages on life's way' indicates a program of development and growth. It also suggests an organic hierarchy: in the beginning, a person is green and indeterminate, but in the fullness of time that person grows into a host of genetic tendencies and temperamental predilections. So, quite naturally, in the beginning a human is drawn to that which is pleasurable, and seeks it out; however, when a person *commits* to being pleased as life's ultimate goal, then the native tension within the human condition achieves a provisional resolution: such a person finds infinite worth in each fleeting, pleasurable bit of finitude; each moment reveals new possibilities for being pleased (from which freely to choose), but the necessity of getting that pleasure continually drives that person on. And, of course, that which pleases is eternally important, and time is measured in terms of how well one is constantly pleased. As Judge William succinctly puts it: '... the essential point is that one wants to enjoy life' (E/O, 2:183).

Why, then, isn't the aesthetic life the solution to the human dilemma of selfhood? The problem with a person getting committed to her or his capacity to have pleasure is *not* that being pleased is somehow intrinsically bad (remember the ongoing enjoyment of our tax collector): the problem is the pursuit itself. The single-minded pleasure-chase ultimately fails to solve the riddle of being human (that is, to satisfy the demands of the 'relata', those opposed dimensions of human experience described by Anti-Climacus).

To see why this is so, consider what a perpetual *commitment* to pleasure might look like. Of course, human beings naturally avoid pain and seek pleasure, but the very notions of both 'pain' and

[3] Cf. C. Stephen Evans's account of Kierkegaard's spheres (2004: 44–51).

'pleasure' are immediately problematic. One person's pain can clearly be another's pleasure (skydiving and NASCAR races will thrill some and torment others), and (extra)ordinary physical pain can be borne, even cheerfully, if it is endured through the lens of some higher purpose (CUP, 1:452–3).[4] Pleasure is an equally vexed category, since self-evident goods are not necessarily pleasure-producing: a banquet hall filled with gustatory treats will delight a hungry person while making a dieter suffer. The pursuit of 'pleasure itself' becomes an impossibility, since the subjective element—that is, a person's particular existential condition—is fundamental to understanding what will actually *constitute* the pleasurable.

Of course, this is the deep insight of the first volume of *Either/Or*, that the pursuit of pleasure, the chasing and the having of good things, paradoxically turns on, indeed turns into, suffering. *Either/Or*, Kierkegaard's first pseudonymous work of 1843, takes the reader through a concatenation of paeans, aphorisms, tales, and meditations about both pleasure and pain; this work is replete with pseudonyms and their characters, several of whom play an important role in what follows. The two volumes are edited by Victor Eremita, who claims to have found a set of papers by an unnamed aesthete, dubbed 'A', as well as letters written to A by someone in the legal profession, Judge (or Assessor) William (or 'Wilhelm', and called 'B' by Eremita). The two volumes (the latter of which also contains a sermon by a Jutland priest) present the reader with two ways of life, each fundamentally inimical to the other in its values, methods, and concerns: A the aesthete approaches his life as a pleasure-seeker, while Judge William understands himself to be constituted by his articulation of, and his making of, choices.

The glittering, heroic, beacon of A's attempted pleasure-life is Mozart's operatic rendition of the Don Juan character, Don Giovanni. Unlike literary treatments of Don Juan, the singing Don Giovanni is able to achieve what it is that A craves: immediate, ongoing, ceaseless and comprehensive sensual satisfaction, shorn of all mediating anticipation and anxiety.

---

[4] To be clear: a person's 'existential condition' does not obviate the reality of physical pain.

This demand for immediacy (in terms of both time and non-mediation) is fundamental to the logic of pleasure: when do we want pleasure? Now. How long do we want it? As long as possible. Accompanying this temporal urgency is the notion that pleasure in its purest form is raw and unmediated: utter ecstasy is not a thought or a memory, or indeed any sort of reflective posture, but absolute erotic saturation in the extended moment.

—Or so the story goes, insofar as such a gloss even makes any sense. Hegel, of course, famously unpacked the concept of 'immediacy' at the outset of the *Phenomenology of Spirit*. Hegel asks his putative (and indeed credulous)[5] interlocutor to consider what the most secure source of knowledge is: what can a person know, indubitably, right now? The initial answer is *sinnliche Gewissheit*, 'sense-certainty': our immediate sensory contact with objects, without any apprehension or reflection, is what provides us with fundamental and unadorned certainty. The shade of G.E. Moore prepares to extend his hands: here is one hand, and here is the other; what could be more obvious, or more immediate?

The problem with this position, of course, becomes clear when each of us tries to experience, or 'seize hold of', our own immediacy. We cannot, because what we 'grasp', when we grasp it, is a *thought* about it, a judgment or a description of that experience. The Hegelian point here is that if there is consciousness of any kind, even a bare 'this-here-now', it is the consciousness that it is because it is structured by concepts. I can only identify 'now' because I am always already oriented by temporal concepts; I identify 'here' on the basis of a prior organization of spatial concepts. 'Immediacy' as absolutely absent of concepts is in this sense a chimera: there is always a conceptual template already in place that makes possible the contours of what we become acquainted with.

Having dialectically 'unpacked' immediacy, we might re-frame the demands of the pleasure-seeker more modestly: perhaps the purest

---

[5] Of this moment in the *Phenomenology* Robert Solomon remarks, 'It is, in other words, the particularly unsophisticated standpoint of common sense—the average incoming college freshman—ready for his first football game and wholly unaware that, before he gets to the stadium, his philosophy instructor will convince him that the world with all its footballs may be nothing but a mere appearance' (1983: 322).

pleasure is focused on sensation and feeling, rather than reflection: the less conceptually mediated and temporally framed a particular experience is, the better. Here Don Giovanni is supremely successful: he is indeed an instance of the 'immediate aesthetic':

> In the Middle Ages much was told about a mountain that is not found on any map; it is called Mount Venus. There sensuousness has its home; there it has its wild pleasures...in this kingdom language has no home, nor the collectedness of thought, not the laborious achievements of reflection; there is heard only the elemental voice of passion, the play of desires, the wild noise of intoxication. There everything is only one giddy round of pleasure. The first born of this kingdom is Don Juan. (E/O, 1:90)

A admires this image of comprehensive sensuality, and deems it perfected when rendered musically: the abstraction of music '...articulates not the particular but the universal in all its universality, and yet it articulates this universality not in the abstraction of reflection but in the concretion of immediacy' (E/O, 1:95).[6] This musical 'concretion of immediacy', however, does not suffer from the usual depletions and lacunae of ordinary sensuality: Don Giovanni is like a 'force of nature' '...which no more wearies of seducing or is through with seducing than the wind with blowing a gale, the sea with rocking, or a waterfall with plunging down from the heights' (E/O, 1:93).

For Don Giovanni, there is no gap between desire and satisfaction (and hence no object of desire); he '...desires and continually goes on desiring and continually enjoys the satisfaction of desire' (E/O, 1:99). But this description of Don Giovanni raises a question about the very nature of desire itself. Desire, of course, is a propositional attitude, one that takes an object: 'I desire X'.[7] Desire also implies lack: I cannot desire a chocolate if I already have one. Furthermore, when I get a chocolate my desire is fulfilled: that desire, so to speak, dies.[8] Of

---

[6] Cf. Sylvia Walsh's excellent account of the musical Don Giovanni (1994: 72).

[7] Or, to use the language of phenomenology, 'desire' is an intentional state that is always directed at something.

[8] This is an observation made by A about the second developmental stage of the immediate erotic (as borne out by the character Papageno in *The Magic Flute*) (E/O, 1:80). A also gives a succinct image of the death of pleasure in the

course, this is Plato's own model of desire,[9] that pleasure is best understood as replenishment: when I am thirsty I drink water and I get pleasure from relieving that need. Of course, when I have drunk my fill my thirst is gone; so too is my pleasure. In order to have more pleasure, I have to have more need—and so the person who pursues the life of pleasure is likened to a leaky jar, necessarily consuming for enjoyment, but also, necessarily, developing a new 'emptiness', a renewed 'hunger' (a notion celebrated by the (mythical) Roman practice of using the vomitorium at a banquet in order to eat more),[10] a new desire that can in turn be pleasurably sated.

Desire, for the aesthete, is therefore a very *un*desirable condition. It is vulnerable: if the object I want is unattainable, I get pain; when I get what I crave, I no longer have that desire, which, of course, is my conduit to pleasure.[11] The trick, evidently, is to have desire without a particular object[12]—an undifferentiated desire—that is equally indifferent to its satisfaction. In this way, pleasure can be maintained throughout. Here is the supreme success of Don Giovanni: his pleasure is ongoing, not a series of yearnings punctuated by dull satiation. Furthermore, all things satisfy him: '... his life is sparkling like the wine with which he fortifies himself; his life is turbulent like the melodies that accompany his joyous repast; he is always jubilant. He needs no preparation, no plan, no time, for he is always ready...' (E/O, 1:101).

'Diapsalmata': 'There are, as is known, insects that die in the moment of fertilization. So it is with all joy: life's highest, most splendid moment of enjoyment is accompanied by death' (E/O, 1:20).

[9] Plato (1987: 66–8).

[10] In his letter to A, Judge William conjures an even more extreme version of this desire-cycle: '... for your rest is a curse ... You are like a starving man whom eating only makes more hungry, a thirsty man whom drinking only makes more thirsty' (E/O, 2:87).

[11] Perhaps this structure of desire, always centered on its own demise, is one reason why death is omnipresent in the sphere of pleasure: the *Symparanekromenoi*, the fellowship of the dead, is only the most obvious instance of this: the death—of desire, of love—is everywhere (E/O, 1:20).

[12] Of course, desire—understood as an intentional mental state—can never be 'contentless'.

Don Giovanni, when rendered in song, is both immediately desirous and satisfied all at once. He has achieved an undifferentiated desire that knows no frustration, and that suffers no gap between the wanting and the having: so considered, Don Giovanni truly does resemble a cataract of water or the wind rather than a human being. Don Juan is sensuality *an sich*: 'Such is his life, effervescing like champagne. And just as the beads in this wine, as it simmers with an internal heat, sonorous with its own melody, rise and continue to rise, just so the lust for enjoyment resonates in the elemental boiling that is his life' (E/O, 1:134).

Reflective Glory

The problem for the aesthete, of course, is that this is art, not life. Don Giovanni the *artistic creation* never reflects, and thus cannot have, for example, better or worse experiences, as human beings most surely do. Only this kind of artwork will allow A to have a glimpse of aesthetic immediacy: A cannot achieve the unselfconsciousness of the character in art, nor can A aspire to this impossible task of non-serial, continuous (and ever-ecstatic) seduction.

Nor does he. A enjoys this unbridled spectacle of immediacy, but A's own version of being wholly unconstrained in his pleasure is realized not in perpetual sensuousness, but in his devotion to, and rapt appreciation of, the music of Mozart:

> Immortal Mozart! You to whom I owe everything—to whom I owe that I lost my mind, that my soul was astounded, that I was terrified at the core of my being—you to whom I owe that I did not go through life without encountering something that could shake me...Indeed, if he were taken away, if his name were blotted out, that would demolish the one pillar that until now has prevented everything from collapsing for me into a boundless chaos, a dreadful nothing. (E/O, 1:49)

This devotion has its advantages. A now has an absolutely meaningful center to his existence; he is, for the moment, no longer prey to the reflective condition that empties life's occupations of their importance: for A, Mozart's music provides absolute worth and significance. A cannot *be* Don Giovanni, but he can steep himself in Mozart's musical rendition of him, and latterly have an aural version of thoroughgoing sensual satisfaction.

The profundity of the Mozart corpus means that A will never be wanting for a pleasurable immersion:

> ... one fears for oneself, that one will lose what made one happy, blissful, rich; one fears for what one loves, that it will suffer in this change, will perhaps appear less perfect, that it will possibly fail to answer the many questions, alas, and then all is lost, the magic is gone, and it can never again be evoked. As for Mozart's music, my soul knows no fear, my confidence no limits. For one thing, what I have understood hitherto is only very little, and enough will always remain, hiding in the shadows of presentiment; for another, I am convinced that if Mozart ever became entirely comprehensible to me, he would then become completely incomprehensible to me. (E/O, 1:60–1)

A can always find amusement in thinking about Mozart's 'musical erotic'; notice, however, that A takes his pleasure in *speculating* about the music, rather than in just being swept up in it. A does chide his reader: 'Listen to Don Giovanni—that is, if you cannot get an idea of Don Giovanni by hearing him, then you never will' (E/O, 1:103), but what about when the curtain falls, or—worse still—what if the bass-baritone sings his role badly? Even though A urges us to 'hear, hear, hear Mozart's Don Giovanni' (E/O, 1:103), A clearly delights in his musicological *investigation*, rather than in simply attending a perform-ance of the opera. We are now very far from Mount Venus, where ' ... language has no home, nor the collectedness of thought, not the laborious achievements of reflection ... ' (E/O, 1:90); in fact, the passion of Don Giovanni, and hence that of A, is now located in *those very labors of reflection*. A musical performance, being realized in a sequence of perpetually vanishing moments, is the perfect medium for expressing immediacy: it is also too evanescent for our committed aesthete. A fine production of *Don Giovanni* is thrilling and remarkable, but that brief theatrical moment has emerged from days of the tedium of rehearsal, replete with missed cues, falling scenery, and false starts; none of this is fit for A's pleasure-consumption. A stellar rendition of *Don Giovanni* is also a fine thing, but that sort of sublime theatrical experience endangers A's potential enjoyment of every subsequent attempt. A dare not lose himself in an actual performance, since it is founded in temporal impermanence, and is ever in thrall to the human talents who attempt it.

A welcome strategy, and one that will take our aesthete as far as he is able to go in his commitment to pleasure, has emerged. If ongoing, immediate pleasure cannot be had, then a reliable source of sensuality will have to do. Mozart's music is dependably awe-inspiring, yet the performances of it are often not; even when they are, they vanish when the house lights come up. *Reflecting* on the wonders of Mozart is, on the other hand, something that A can always do. A's thoughts and imaginings are his best resource for finding and maintaining pleasure.

A's move to what we can call the 'reflective aesthetic' opens up a new, and seemingly more feasible, pleasure-terrain. The practitioner of the reflective aesthetic finds pleasure in his thoughts and imaginings, all of which can be summoned for the aesthete's entertainment in a moment's stroke. Of course, the careful pleasure-tender will be sure to have a variety of delights on hand, since boredom is, as A puts it, '. . . the root of all evil' (E/O, 1:286). One way to stave off boredom is to adopt the 'rotation method': rather than restlessly move from place to place, why not just plant an endless array of new crops in the same soil? (E/O, 1:292). The imagination is boundless, and the clever aesthete will always manage to have some new delight on hand, something to anticipate, to dream about, and to savor.

Here the resemblance to our faithful tax collector is striking. The pleasure that the tax collector takes 'in everything' (FT, 32) is *also* evidently inexhaustible—whether dreaming of stew for supper or planning an extravagant building project, the tax collector is always already immersed in the pleasure of his existence; whatever it brings to him, he takes it up as something to be relished.

Is this what A the aesthete has achieved? Will the rotation method work?

Certainly, A now governs an unfettered pleasure-field: 'Real enjoyment consists not in what one enjoys but in the idea' (E/O, 1:31). Here resourcefulness is crucial: A must manage his imaginatively constructed desires and their fulfillment in such a way that he both avoids boredom and makes use of the material to hand. 'The more a person limits himself, the more resourceful he becomes. A solitary prisoner for life is extremely resourceful; to him a spider can be a source of great amusement' (E/O, 1:292).

So, what of this strategy? The crop rotator is never at the behest of tedium or accident, because everything can be transmuted by the 'art of the arbitrary':

> One enjoys something totally accidental; one considers the whole of existence [*Tilværelse*] from this standpoint; one lets its reality run aground on this. I shall give an example. There was a man whose chatter I was obliged to listen to . . . On the verge of despair, I suddenly discovered that the man perspired exceptionally much when he spoke. This perspiration now absorbed my attention. I watched how the pearls of perspiration collected on his forehead, then united in a rivulet, slid down his nose, and ended in a quivering globule that remained suspended at the end of his nose. From that moment on, everything was changed; I could even have the delight of encouraging him to commence his philosophical instruction just in order to watch the perspiration on his brow and on his nose. (E/O, 1: 299)

A now occupies an impossible position. Once his imagination is charged with transmuting the stuff of experience into the content for desire *it can no longer really provide that content*. Actual pleasure flows from spontaneous desire, but the goal of the Rotation Method is in fact to protect A from the vicissitudes of desire. If every experience (or indeed every fantasy-experience) is equally able to provide delight, then no particular episode can have more significance for A than any other: behold, a sweaty nose can delight A as much as a beautiful body can! A's attempt at crop rotation ends in being leveled. Just as the uncommitted denizens of the Present Age are forever wandering from one enticing reflection to another, with everything (and hence nothing) being of interest, so too is A condemned to invest every moment with a merely putative pleasure.

The 'reflective aesthetic' has an initial plausibility that the immediate aesthetic does not, yet it suffers from an actual internal contradiction. The reflective aesthete wants his entire existence-condition to be comprehensively pleasurable (as it is for the fictional Don Giovanni), but that demand violates the inherent logic of preference that is the nature of desire itself: *this*, says desire, *and certainly not that*. As A observes in the 'Diapsalmata': 'If I were to wish for something, I would wish not for wealth or power but for the passion of possibility, for the eye, eternally young, eternally ardent, that sees possibility everywhere. Pleasure disappoints; possibility does not' (E/O, 1:41).

Untrammeled possibility loses in potency what it gains in ubiquity: the significance of satisfied desire is lost.

The Seduction

But A's reflective gambit is ever inventive, and new refinements of this strategy emerge. What better way to tend and exploit the lure of possibility than in the art of seduction? The final section of *Either/Or I* is an account, kept as a diary, of Johannes the Seducer and his diabolically ingenious erotic method. The diary was found among the papers of A, who tells the reader in an introductory note that he has copied out these entries (as well as some of the victim's anguished letters) on the sly. Johannes records, in elaborate, lyrical detail, his seduction of a young woman, seventeen-year-old Cordelia Wahl. Johannes writes that Cordelia 'has no real conception of the erotic' (E/O, 1:382), and indeed she will serve as the canvas on which his own image of *himself* as the beloved emerges.

Johannes is clear about his goal for the girl: 'I am seeking immediacy' (E/O, 1:381). Of course, the 'immediacy' he wants is one free of both boredom and frustration; his experience must be stage-managed. That managerial method is poetry: Johannes will ignite and then carefully tend an *actual* erotic passion—Cordelia's—and Johannes's pleasure is thus produced by observing the deception unfold, and the rapt joy of reviewing his own written account of the affair. The goal is not (immediately) the sexual possession of Cordelia, but to inspire her, of her own free will, to give herself over to Johannes, and thus to provide Johannes with his poetic material.

Johannes's erotic satisfaction is not the result of the seduction itself; as usual, the satisfaction of desire is its death. Johannes makes this chilling comment towards the end of his erotic adventure: 'How Cordelia preoccupies me! And yet the time will soon be over ... as soon as a girl has devoted herself completely, the whole thing is finished' (E/O, 1:435). The actual sexual encounter—as fleeting as the night itself—brings Johannes's narrative to an abrupt end: 'Why cannot such a night last longer? ... But now it is finished, and I never want to see her again. When a girl has given away everything, she is weak, she has lost everything ... ' (E/O, 1:445). But Johannes can now turn his full attention to the genuine source of his ongoing enjoyment, his poetical rendition of Cordelia's love for him, complete with endless variety and embellishment. Here is the concluding thought of the diary: 'Yet it would really be worth knowing whether or not one could poetize oneself out of a girl in such a way as to make her so proud that she imagined it was she who was bored with the relationship. It could be an interesting epilogue, which in and by itself could have psychological interest and besides that furnish one with many erotic observations' (E/O, 1:445).

Johannes the Seducer is a parasite on Cordelia's actual experience, and his poetry is that of the voyeur. A so tells his reader in his anxious preamble to the diary: '... he egotistically enjoyed personally that which in part actuality has given to him and which in part he himself has used to fertilize actuality... he then enjoyed the situation and himself in the situation... he continually needed actuality as the occasion, as an element... actuality was drowned in the poetic' (E/O, 1:305). But what about Cordelia herself? A remarks, 'For him, individuals were merely for stimulation; he discarded them as trees shake off their leaves—he was rejuvenated, the foliage withered' (E/O, 1:308). Johannes argues that as an aesthete he has indeed been 'faithful' to Cordelia: 'In my relation to Cordelia, have I been continually faithful to my pact? That is, *my pact with the esthetic*, for it is that which makes me strong—that I continually have the idea on my side... Plainly and simply to deceive a girl, for that I certainly would not have the stamina; but the fact that the idea is present in motion, that I am acting in its service... this gives me rigorousness towards myself ...' (E/O, 1:437, emphasis mine). Johannes is faithful to the poeticized erotic narrative which features a character named Cordelia, and reckless of the girl herself.

The *actual* Cordelia, however, is crucial, for it is her passion that anchors Johannes's poetry in the immediate, real world. Here the finite once again wears flesh; unlike the endless fantasy-vista of the Rotation Method, Johannes's project has a foothold in an unfolding sensual event. His experience is focused on how Cordelia experiences him; his identity is, in the moment, determined by her view of him: Johannes is what he is in her eyes, and that identity becomes the substance for his own fantastic lyrical account. Notice how near this draws to the condition of the (fictional) Don Giovanni, who is perpetually, endlessly pleased with himself (just as a waterfall might be poetically rendered as an ongoing joyous cascade, needing nothing beyond the effervescence of its own phenomenal reality); Johannes takes pleasure in the version of himself as seen by his victim, and in his own recording (and presumably re-reading) of this version: 'My Cordelia, I am in love with myself, people say of me . . . I am in love with myself. And why? Because I am in love with you; for you I love and you alone and everything that truly belongs to you, and thus I love myself because this self of mine belongs to you . . . ' (E/O, 1:404).

The Seducer, like A (and, as we will see momentarily, the Unhappiest One), is committed to recollection: in recollecting his erotic adventure, the Seducer can translate the actual into an ideal possibility. Both A and the Seducer are estranged from actuality, although in very different ways: A's 'rotation' and his life in recollection do not take up the world as an inherently meaningful place; the Seducer also does not deal with the world, or other people, *as such*, but always as devices in an elaborate game: 'One should always make preparatory studies; everything must be properly arranged . . . ' (E/O, 1:342); once arranged, then the simulacrum begins: 'Now, I have made many declarations of love in my life . . . this declaration must be made in an altogether distinctive way. Primarily what I must drum into myself is that the whole thing is merely a simulated move . . . ' (E/O, 1:371); when Cordelia's passion is aroused, the Seducer can feed from it: 'I can always make use of mood, and the girl's beautiful longing has really stirred me' (E/O, 1:384). Unlike A's rotation of imaginings, the Seducer really does have a tentative foothold in (someone else's) immediate experience. Has he fared any better than A?

The Seducer's use of actual, temporally realized human experience has a curious and revealing subtext. When Johannes describes his erotic scheme, he often uses the explicit language of faith, using the terms that will later[13] be used to characterize our pleasure-filled tax collector, and indeed Abraham himself. Johannes describes the role of Governance in his project: 'There is a higher Governance that comes to the aid of love . . . ' (E/O, 1:357); he tells us that Cordelia's soul must discover 'the infinite', and that this transition will be 'a leap'

---

[13] *Either/Or* was published on February 20, 1843; *Fear and Trembling* appeared on October 16, 1843.

(E/O, 1:391); most tellingly, Johannes claims that he will help Cordelia to achieve 'erotic inwardness' by way of a 'double-movement' (E/O, 1:386–7). Of course, the double-movement is central to the life of faith, and it is the subject of *Fear and Trembling*: '[Abraham] . . . believed—that God would not demand Isaac. He was no doubt surprised then at the outcome, but by a *double movement* he has regained his original condition and therefore received Isaac more joyfully than the first time' (FT, 29, emphasis mine).

Recall that faith's 'epistemic flexibility' is that ability to move between the absolute parameters of a finite condition and God's boundless possibilities—'for God everything is possible . . . ' (FT, 39); Abraham knows that he cannot both sacrifice Isaac and keep him, and he is infinitely resigned to that fact; however, he has faith that God can offer an (impossible) possibility: 'He replies then: "God himself will provide the lamb for the burnt offering, my son!" From this one sees the *double movement* in Abraham's soul . . . If Abraham had merely resigned Isaac and done no more, then he would have offered an untruth, for he indeed *knows* that God demands Isaac for a sacrifice, and he *knows* that he is at this moment ready to sacrifice him. After having made this movement, he has at every moment made the next one . . . by virtue of the absurd it is indeed possible that God could do something entirely different' (FT, 105, emphasis mine).

What manner, then, of 'double movement' is Johannes the erotics-artist proposing? Here is his explanation:

> A double-movement is necessary in relation to Cordelia. If I just keep on retreating before her superior force, it would be very possible that the erotic in her would become too dissolute and lax for the deeper womanliness to be able to hypostatize itself . . . I could use either conversation to inflame her or letters to cool her off, or vice versa. The latter is preferable in every way. I then enjoy her most extreme moments. When she has received a letter, when its sweet poison has entered her blood, then a word is sufficient to make her love burst forth. At the next moment, irony and hoarfrost make her doubtful . . . My personal presence will prevent ecstasy. If I am only present in a letter, then she can easily cope with me; to some extent, she mistakes me for a more universal creature who dwells in her love . . . (E/O, 1:386)

Johannes has deftly—and perversely—counterfeited the double movement that faith achieves. The 'movement' here is between Johannes's 'inflammatory' letters, his words that inspire Cordelia's boundless yearning, and the harsh light of quotidian day, filled with 'irony and hoarfrost'. The more Cordelia falls in love with Johannes's specter of words, the harder she will attempt to reconcile the fantasy with actuality, to 'express the sublime in the pedestrian', just as our tax collector does (FT, 34). The tax collector's faith gives him what Johannes de silentio calls 'inwardness'; Cordelia too will, according to Johannes, achieve 'erotic inwardness' from this program of double-movements: but this form of 'inwardness' merely caricatures the faithful life. Cordelia moves from a staged narrative of love to a performance intended to manage that story; any reconciliation she fashions of the 'infinitely possible' and the finite 'facts' will vanish as the sun rises on her defloration.

What can we say of Johannes's erotic practice—that it is vile, depraved? Of course. But does this strategy *work* for Johannes by providing him with a stable source of meaning? No, it does not, and for an obvious reason: his seductions seriously misunderstand the human frame, namely, the boundaries of the finite and the limits of time. If, as de silentio says of the tax collector, 'Temporality, finitude is what it is all about' (FT, 42), then the Seducer has lost himself to one great ever-recurring round, greased with lies and out of touch with the carnality on which it depends.

This point is made more directly when the Seducer appears again in *Stages on Life's Way* (1845) in 'In Vino Veritas'. The occasion is an impromptu banquet, and the gathered aesthetes intend to drink, feast, and make speeches (Plato's *Symposium* provides both structure and a template for the theme).[14] The five participants—Victor Eremita, a Young Man, Constantin Constantius, the Fashion Designer, and the Seducer—gather to enjoy a 'perfect banquet': as the Seducer puts it, 'there was only one who was able to arrange a banquet, and that was the tablecloth that spreads itself and sets everything out if one merely says: "Spread yourself"' (SLW, 22). The banquet must appear at once in all its glamorous opulence and then, at its conclusion, be instantly

[14] We will have more to say about the *Symposium* in the Coda.

taken away. As Victor Eremita exclaims (as a good aesthete would), 'Anything that is good must be that immediately, for "immediately" is the most divine of categories...' (SLW, 23). As the banquet begins, each in turn gives a speech, not about *eros*, but about women; the last speaker is, of course, Johannes the Seducer. He argues that women should be regarded as 'bait' to be eaten, while avoiding the trap of marriage. Johannes concludes: '... what else is a woman but a dream, and yet the highest reality. This is how the devotee of erotic love sees her and in the moment of seduction leads her and is led by her *outside of time*, where as an illusion she belongs. With a husband she becomes temporal, and he through her' (SLW, 80, emphasis mine). Here Johannes explicitly denies the constitutive power of time over human creatures: but notice what happens next. The party is decisively over, and as Constantin throws down his goblet the doors open to '... forces of annihilation; we saw that demolition crew ready to destroy everything—a memento that instantly changed the participants into refugees' (SLW, 81). Johannes can repudiate time, and seek to outwit it by dwelling in serial seductions, but it is still the case that he too is temporal, and his time runs on, and out, without establishing the significance of selfhood.[15]

Now we may ask a question that was suggested earlier: why does the Seducer make A so apprehensive? For frighten him he does. Here are the first lines of A's introduction to the diary: 'Hide from myself, I cannot; I can hardly control the anxiety that grips me at this moment when I decide in my own interest to make an accurate clean copy of the hurried transcript I was able to obtain at the time only in the greatest haste and with great uneasiness' (E/O, 1:303). A's nervousness is not merely about his intrusion into the Seducer's private papers; the content gives him pause, too. 'Terrible it is for [Cordelia]; more terrible it will be for him—this I can conclude from the fact that I myself can scarcely control the anxiety that grips me every time I think about the affair' (E/O, 1:310). This anxiety, and the

---

[15] In making this very point about Johannes, Perkins delightfully observes, 'I conclude with one other statement, slightly expanded, about banquets, the well-known line of Auntie Mame: "Life is a banquet, but most poor suckers"—Athenians and Copenhageners alike, even if they have banqueted all night—"are starving to death"' (1997: 83–102).

intimations of the stirrings of conscience, may be an indication that A sees the hopelessness of the aesthetic life.

The Happiest Unhappiness

But A is not done yet; his reflective powers have not yet exhausted themselves. As much as A would like to make the Rotation Method work, or to construct a residual practice that is able to escape leveling, he cannot. A central strategy[16] emerges: A will embrace his misery; he will succeed by being miserable. The 'Diapsalmata' which begins *Either/Or* opens with this theme: 'What is a poet? An unhappy person who conceals profound anguish in his heart but whose lips are so formed that as sighs and cries pass over them they sound like beautiful music' (E/O, 1:19). The idea that even the sounds of torture (A's reference is to the bronze bull of Phalaris, in which his victims '... were slowly tortured over a slow fire; their screams could not reach the tyrant's ears to terrify him; to him they sounded like sweet music') can be transformed into aural loveliness reaches completion in the episode of 'The Unhappiest One'.

And who is 'The Unhappiest One'? This is the question taken up by the *Symparanekromenoi*, the (literally, in cobbled-together Greek) 'fellowship of the dead'. The editor, Victor Eremita, gives us a copy of an address (presumably given by A) to the *Symparanekromenoi* at one of their 'meetings on Fridays' (all-too suggestive of the penitential communion on Friday, for which Kierkegaard composed several sermons)[17] in which a competition is proposed: how to find the 'Unhappiest One'? There is a grave in England that is so marked, but no corpse was found within; surely the *Symparanekromenoi* can, 'like crusaders', make a pilgrimage to this empty tomb and decide who in fact is the unhappiest human being (E/O, 1:219).

---

[16] This address to the *Symparanekromenoi* is, in *Either/Or I*, literally central; as in a Platonic dialogue, *Either/Or I* provides an oblique answer to the riddle of the aesthetic sphere in the middle of the text. Please note Judge William's characterization of A's self-fashioning as 'the unhappiest one' on p. 82, fn 72.

[17] Cf. WA, 109–88. The second of these discourses (published on November 14, 1849) features the tax collector from Luke 18:13; we will have more to say about him in the Fourth Movement.

Some competitors are eliminated right away. Anyone unhappy about the prospect of death is disqualified: '. . . we, like the Roman soldiers, do not fear death; we know a worse calamity, and first and last, above all—it is to live' (E/O, 1:220). A invites everyone who has ever lived to compete for the title, and several august figures appear: Antigone, Niobe, and Job are all considered, and ultimately rejected. A reminds the *Symparanekromenoi* that Hegel (in the *Phenomenology of Spirit*) describes an unsettling notion, the 'unhappy consciousness'; A then glosses this idea: 'The unhappy one is the person who in one way or another has his ideal, the substance of his life, the plenitude of his consciousness, his essential nature, outside himself' (E/O, 1:222).

So far A's version is fairly accurate, but he will soon deviate from Hegel's thinking in a crucial way. Just to review Hegel's own account: in the *Phenomenology of Spirit*,[18] the 'Unhappy Consciousness' is a stage

[18] Hegel's 'unhappy consciousness' (1977) is a dialectical outcome of the path that consciousness has traveled from the awakening of 'consciousness' to 'self-consciousness', and so to the conflict of self-consciousness attempting to establish its authority over another self-consciousness: thus the 'lord and bondsman' figure emerges. The lord, of course, has power over the bondsman, but he is also dependent on the slave; the bondsman is (relatively) independent in his work, but still enslaved. These aspects of the relation between the lord and bondsman are recapitulated in Hegel's account of the unhappy consciousness. The unhappy consciousness, Hegel claims, emerges dialectically out of the historical movements of Stoicism and Skepticism. In Stoicism I am real and rational, and must submit to the vagaries of existence; in Skepticism I am transient, confused: these 'vagaries' *are* my reality, and I reject any idea of having knowledge (and thus acquire a kind of power over it). In both of these moments I seek mastery, and in both I also submit: in the unhappy consciousness this duality is embraced. The unhappy consciousness turns out to be an internal version of the lord–bondsman relationship. (Self-)consciousness can now only find unity in its thoughts of a divine realm, thoughts which are constantly contradicted by the harsh realities of everyday life. Hegel (obliquely) reviews various religions that display unhappy consciousness: the 'unchangeable'—God—is something other than us, and indeed the 'unchangeable' does assume an individual form (that of Christ). The penitent seeker wants communion with the unchangeable—with God—and sets about to scourge the flesh in order to so do. But this union cannot happen, and the seeker is ultimately made to feel alien and inadequate. Hegel's triumphant conclusion is that the unhappy consciousness has failed to recognize that *consciousness itself* is the conceptual source of both notions, and thus it embodies *both* the changeable and unchangeable: consciousness can now recognize itself in the 'unchangeable'. In

in the development of human consciousness in which human consciousness is torn between what Hegel calls 'natural existence'—the life of relationships, the exigencies of the human body—and the life of the spirit. The story of St. Augustine's life-journey is an excellent example of Hegel's 'unhappy consciousness'. As Augustine sees it, on the one hand he can be understood as eternal and unchanging—his soul that belongs to God—but the other part of Augustine's 'nature', his bodily appetites and urges, is unessential and mutable (not to mention sinful).[19] Hegel's solution to this self-divide lies (of course, given his dialectical approach) in the framework of the problem itself. What (self-)consciousness needs to understand is that *both* aspects of the self belong to it: consciousness is *itself* the source and author of the essential, eternal, and unchanging dimension of human thought. Instead, consciousness 'takes flight to the Deity' without recognizing that it is itself the source of this notion of the Godhead. This alienation, says Hegel, can be overcome when human consciousness sees that it is itself the very site where the infinite is 'realized' in the finite.[20]

A's peroration to the *Symparanekromenoi* initially cleaves to Hegel's notion that human consciousness is unhappy because its 'ideal', as A puts it, is 'outside himself': but notice how A then shifts the issue: 'The unhappy one is the person who is always absent, one obviously never present to himself ... But one is absent when one is in either *past or future time*' (E/O, 1:222, emphasis mine). The 'unhappy one' as rendered by A is a person who is *temporally* alienated from himself. A is now working on a very different problem from Hegel, who—in the *Phenomenology*—is proposing to negotiate the way in which human consciousness is dialectically riven: by thinking differently about itself, human consciousness can actually become a new, more highly

---

this final movement, self-consciousness regains the insight it lost in Stoicism, namely, the higher reality of the life of thought, now married to its material life.

[19] As Augustine remarks in the *Confessions*, 'O Lord ... now that I have the evidence of my own misery to prove to me how displeasing I am to myself, you are my light and joy. It is you whom I love and desire, so that I am ashamed of myself and cast myself aside and choose you instead ...' (1961: 207).

[20] Hegel (1977: 138–9).

rational, entity (right now). But A's unhappy ones are not going to be corrected by enlightened thinking: it is indeed their way of (mis)conceiving themselves that has ruined their lives, but that ruin has to do with the way in which they existentially occupy time, and the perverse pleasure-device that this way of life has created. There will be no dialectical re-framing for A or his fellow aesthetes; only by means of a leap (*Spring*) can these aesthetes find a new commitment, and thus a new way of living (an event that happens well beyond the borders of *Either/Or* I).

But the circuit of despair must be completed before such a leap can be executed. The question remains: who will win the laurel of the 'Unhappiest One', and on what grounds? A provides us with a necessary condition—'Recollection is above all the distinctive element of the unhappy ones...' (E/O, 1:223)—and a chilling example: '...imagine a person who had had no childhood himself... but who now, for example, by becoming a teacher of children, discovered all the beauty in childhood and now wanted to recollect his own childhood... he would discover backwards the meaning of that which was past for him and which he nevertheless wanted to recollect in all its meaning' (E/O, 1:224). Thus the winning formula: '...it is recollection that prevents him from becoming present in his hope and it is hope that prevents him from becoming present in his recollection...' (E/O, 1:225).

The 'Unhappiest One' is indeed 'the unhappy lover of recollection', forever remembering what was not, and hoping for what cannot be: and, of course, taking pleasure in this lament. Here we arrive at the distillation of the aesthetic stage of life: embracing one's misery in order to insure pleasure. What a gambit! If the aesthete can enjoy the extremity of suffering, then pleasure has once again become comprehensive.[21] Everything thus occasions delight, because recollection can govern the heart-piercing content of every moment. This insight is uttered early on in the 'Diapsalmata': 'To live in recollection is the most perfect life imaginable; recollection is more richly satisfying than all actuality, and it has a security that no actuality possesses.

---

[21] As Judge William remarks to A: '...that in which you find your satisfaction is absolute dissatisfaction' (E/O, 2:202).

A recollected life relationship has already passed into eternity and has no temporal interest anymore' (E/O, 1:32).

A's third address to the *Symparanekromenoi* reveals this ultimate aesthetic coping strategy: the Unhappiest One wants what he cannot have, and does not want what he can have. The Unhappiest One's past is reflectively constructed, and his memory is a yearning for the past immediacy—actual experiences—that he never had. The future is already seen as unsatisfactory because it, like the past, cannot have this content: '... he is continually recollecting that for which he should hope, because he has already encompassed it and the future in thought, and he recollects what he has experienced instead of hoping for it. Thus, what he is hoping for lies behind him; what he recollects lies ahead of him. His life is not backwards but is turned the wrong way in two directions' (E/O, 1:225). He can only hope for what he has already been, and that is nothing. The aesthete's pleasure-ruse *seems* to end in a kind of annihilation, thus effectively settling the question of selfhood: but this final ploy only underscores the actual, pressing question of becoming a self, one that the aesthete has yet to answer.

A has taken a fantastical pleasure-odyssey in which a number of strategies have come to ruin, from the rotation method in which all things potentially delight (obviating, of course, the distinction between what a person *actually* wants from what she does not want; the very same experience can be gripping or meaningless, depending on A's subjective assessment) to the preserved, aspic-happiness of recollection, to, at last, the bitter triumph of the Unhappiest One: 'But what am I saying—"the unhappiest"? I ought to say "the happiest" ... See, language breaks down, and thought is confused, for who indeed is the happiest but the unhappiest and who the unhappiest but the happiest, and what is life but madness, and faith but foolishness, and hope but a staving off of the evil day, and love but vinegar in the wound' (EO, 1:230). In his efforts to commit to pleasure, A ends up finding his substance and meaning in unhappiness.

How did A arrive at this wrecked condition? Our tax collector, still cheerfully making his rounds in the streets of Copenhagen, comes bracingly into view. Surely *his* is the life that the aesthete wanted to secure: a joyful absorption in the unfolding moment, finding significance and delight in ordinary existence as it is lived—as rats scurry and children play, and as the manifold occupations and demands of each temporally driven finite engagement, from singing hymns to bookkeeping, become the embodiment of the infinite worth of these humble tasks. The tax collector ambles on, sublimely and merrily located in the finite time that is his life.

But not so for A. A's efforts to secure himself through pleasure (and on that basis to establish a coherent life) are continually dispersed, bouncing between pleasures, real and imagined. A splits himself in nostalgia and regret, looking on at himself as he makes poetry out of deception. As another pseudonym, Judge William, famously remarks, 'his soul is like a plot of ground in which all sorts of herbs are planted . . . his self consists in this multifariousness' (E/O, 2:225).[22] The good judge also takes note of the particular danger in which the Unhappiest One finds himself: 'This may be the place to discuss briefly a life-view that is so very pleasing to you . . . It amounts to nothing less than this, that to sorrow is indeed the real meaning of life, and to be the unhappiest one is the supreme happiness.' Judge William then issues a warning: 'At first sight, this view does not seem to be an esthetic view of life, because enjoyment cannot be its watchword. But it is not ethical either; it is situated at the perilous point at which the esthetic is to pass over into the ethical . . .' (E/O, 2:232).[23]

That 'perilous point'—the jumping-off point, if you will—is where we will leave A.

Perhaps his struggles have not been in vain; after all, the aesthete was initially drawn out of his leveled condition by the seductions of the life of pleasure; now that a first life-commitment has been made, A might choose to make the 'leap' to another life-commitment. Clearly, this first stage, the provisional self that is forged in the 'aesthetic' sphere, cannot maintain itself: hence Judge William's thought that A really has exhausted the possibilities for the aesthetic stage of existence. A, of course, does not understand the depth of

[22] Cf. Constantin Constantius's account of the aesthetic personality (R, 154).

[23] Judge William goes on to accuse A: 'Here, too, you come with your pretension, the gist of which is neither more nor less than that you are the unhappiest one. And yet it is undeniable that this thought is the proudest and the most defiant that can arise in the mind of a human being' (E/O, 2:236).

this crisis; an external, observing eye is needed to explain how it is that the life of pleasure has collapsed into pain. Judge William—A's older friend of many years[24]—is that observer, and his assessment of how, and why, the aesthetic sphere has failed is our next investigation.

[24] Judge William is seven years older than A (E/O, 2:87).

4

Third Movement

The Pleasures of Choice

'But what is it, then, that I choose—is it this or that? No, for I choose absolutely....and what is that? It is myself in my eternal validity.' (E/O, 2:214)

The Marital-Ethical

What next? A's decisions about how best to secure ongoing pleasure for himself have come to ruin. The possibilities for the aesthetic life have run out, but one capacity remains available to A: he can still make choices about his life. As Judge William puts it: '...what a person chooses is always important. It is important that he choose properly, test himself...' (E/O, 2:157). Pleasure vanishes with the grasping, but the ability to articulate, discriminate, and choose is always available to A; in fact, his struggles with the aesthetic stage of life have always had to do with *choosing* what will provide the most consistent gratification. Now a new life-stage comes into view: a bold existential 'leap' (*Spring*) to a new framework for living is possible. A may come to see himself not as defined by his ability to be comprehensively pleased, but by his capacity to choose. Judge William (or 'Assessor Wilhelm', or B)[1] is our redoubtable (and incredibly prolix) voice for the ethical stage or 'sphere' of existence.

Again, the name of this way of life can mislead. Of course, a life defined by the human power to choose will certainly have to do with

---

[1] 'Assessor' is closer to the Danish, but the title of 'Judge' does capture the articulating, discriminating, and choosing that is central to his sphere of existence. See Pattison (2005: 91); also E/O, 2:323.

conventional ethical problems (and dilemmas; more of that moment-arily), but 'the ethical' stage of life is fundamentally concerned with conceptual limning and framing. Recall Hegel's account of the 'Unhappy Consciousness': if only self-consciousness can come to see that it is itself the source of its alienation from the Godhead, then that alienation vanishes (and is replaced with a new set of dialogical tensions). Judge William, in a lengthy letter to A, urges him to think clearly about his dissolute existence, and to conceive of his life-project in a new way. The scolding, long-windedness of Judge William's address is part of the point: as the good judge puts it, '. . . I am reluctant to miss the opportunity of addressing you in the more admonishing and urgent tone appropriate to the epistolary form' (E/O, 2:5). The emergency is, of course, the wreck that A's life has become: 'Your life will amount to nothing but tentative efforts at living' (E/O, 2:7). Judge William is clearly fond of A, and although he admires the tortured elegance of A's intellect, he wants A to think again about how he conducts his life.

The good judge begins with two assertions. First, the human frame is constituted by choice: a person's situation—bodily, economic, familial, professional, erotic—is what it is because of that person's history of choosing. Even the accidents and mishaps that punctuate every life have the qualities and characteristics that they do because they have been perceived and managed in a particular way, and those particulars are, of course, chosen. Judge William asserts, with consid-erable relish: ' . . . I am not a logician, and I have only one category, but I assure you that it is the choice of both my heart and my thought, my soul's delight and my salvation—I go back to the significance of choosing' (E/O, 2:213).

Lest A misunderstand this veneration of choice (the notion of 'choice' always serving as shorthand for the articulation, discrimin-ation, and the ultimate making of distinctions that serious choosing involves[2]) as praise for the occupation of an utterly self-absorbed agent, Judge William insists that a person only emerges from an infantile kind of self-involvement when he understands himself[3] as a

[2] Cf. Charles Taylor (1985: 15–44).

[3] For Judge William, the 'ethical person' is a male, since only men (to echo Aristotle) have the full complement of the rational capacity. Here is a typical

chooser; only then is that person fully equipped to enter and to participate in the civic order.

Judge William's observation is apt: a person can hardly become a fully fledged social and civic participant until that person knows who, and what, he or she is:

> The person who has ethically chosen and found himself possesses himself defined in his entire concretion. He then possesses himself as an individual who had these capacities, these passions, these inclinations, these habits, who is subject to these external influences, who is influenced in one direction thus and in another way thus. Here he then possesses himself as a task in such a way that it is chiefly to order, shape, temper, inflame, control—in short, to produce an evenness in the soul, a harmony, which is the fruit of the personal virtues. Here the objective for his activity is himself, but nevertheless not arbitrarily determined, for *he possesses himself as a task that has been assigned him, even though it became his by choosing* . . . The self that is the objective is not only a personal self but *a social, a civic self*. He then possesses himself as a task in an activity whereby he engages in the affairs of life as this specific personality. His task is not to form himself but *to act*. (E/O, 2:262–3, emphasis mine)

Notice that Judge William emphasizes the 'task' assigned to each person, one that directs the actions of an agent wholly wedded—indeed, utterly understood in terms of—a life of civic involvement and action. A person committed to the ethical life is no drifting dreamer, preoccupied with imagination's delightful (or neurotically frightful) confections: no, the ethical person takes action in the world.

This is the first—and by no means the last—way in which Judge William bears a striking resemblance to our tax collector. Recall that the tax collector ' . . . belongs entirely to the world; no bourgeois philistine could belong to it more . . . he goes about his work' (FT, 32).

---

declaration: ' . . . even if it behooves the woman to be silent in the congregation and not to be occupied with scholarship and art, what is said about marriage ought essentially to be such that it meets with her approval. It does not follow that she is supposed to know how to evaluate everything critically—that kind of reflection is not suitable for her . . . ' (SLW, 91). Of this posture, Céline Léon remarks, 'Should the conclusion that a woman cannot be good/ethical in the same way as a man not complicate the stance of the male ready for union within that sphere?' (2008: 111).

So too does Judge William go about his work; he is, if you like, who he is in the work that he does.

My portrait of the hard-working Judge William is missing something, however. Yes, the ethical stage or sphere of life has to do with a self that is forged by a commitment to the capacity to choose: but the ethical life, so described, sounds clinically judicial. Judge William's particular understanding of the civic life is, however, hardly dispassionate: Judge William is himself fiercely erotic, and the vehicle for his ardor is the institution of marriage.

Yes! Judge William is a zealous celebrant of the married estate, and he wants A to recognize that he, not A (or, more specifically, Johannes the Seducer), has achieved what has eluded A, the pleasures of an erotically satisfied condition.

The initial section title of the second volume of *Either/Or* tells us all we need to know about the ardor of Judge William: his first essay is called 'The Aesthetic Validity of Marriage'. Already we can hear a defense being mounted: not only is married life superior to the groping of immediate desire; marriage actually manages to carry on, and elevate, the urge for pleasure that initially motivates the aesthetic stage or sphere of life: 'So you see the nature of the task I have set for myself: to show that romantic love can be united with and exist in marriage—indeed, that *marriage is its true transfiguration*' (E/O, 2:31, emphasis mine). Judge William declares that marriage is the source of a sustained emotional pleasure, one that is 'higher'—that is, more consistently successful—than the immediate satisfactions of yearning and seduction.

But why is *marriage* the signature choice of the ethical stage of life? It certainly is for Judge William; as he exults in *Stages on Life's Way* (in another exceedingly long discourse, 'Some Reflections on Marriage in Answer to Objections'), '... marriage is and remains the most *important voyage of discovery* a human being undertakes ... praised be marriage, praised be everyone who speaks in its honor ... everything revolves around *little things that the divine element in marriage nevertheless transforms by a miracle into something significant for the believer*' (SLW, 90, emphasis mine). Again, the tax collector comes to mind: he too is pleasurably absorbed in the smallest details of the world around him, from watching the new omnibuses roll by to smoking a pipe. For our tax collector, all things teem with significance; evidently, Judge William's marriage enables him to take up his daily life in much the same way.

In order to see why being married expresses the essential task of the ethical, we need to consider Judge William's analysis of the aesthetic life. He argues that he has seen, and understood, what A in his tormented throes cannot: A is attempting to establish himself as a self by committing to pleasure: 'Every human being, no matter how slightly gifted he is, however subordinate his position in life may be, has a natural need to formulate a life-view, a conception of the meaning of life and its purpose. The person who lives aesthetically does that, and the popular expression heard in all ages and from various stages is this: One must enjoy life' (E/O, 2:179). Judge William hastens to add that A's profound, highly reflective pursuit of enjoyment should not be confused with the work of mere amateurs: 'You may be thinking that I ought to be sufficiently courteous to treat you as an artist and tacitly ignore the bunglers... you do nevertheless have something in common with them, and something very essential—namely, a life-view...' (E/O, 2:180). The Judge produces an elaborate taxonomy of the ways in which a person can devote him or herself to 'enjoying life': a person may embrace physical beauty, and '... for a short time plumes herself or himself on her or his beauty, but it soon deceives them' (E/O, 2:181). Some seekers of enjoyment find their pleasure-source in cultural trappings ('... wealth, honors, noble birth'), while others find meaning in some ability they have, a talent for something: 'Satisfaction in life, enjoyment, is sought in the unfolding of this talent' (E/O, 2:183); still, as the Judge points out, all of these seekers find their pleasure-condition externally: even the person taking pleasure in her native talent did not create that ability (E/O, 2:180).

Judge William pauses to consider what happens when a person commits to chasing, and attempting to satisfy, desire: 'But desire per se is a multiplicity, and thus it is easy to see that this life splits up into a boundless multiplicity...' (E/O, 2:183); he imagines a person who, like the emperor Nero, has nearly endless material resources for the pursuit: 'Now he snatches at pleasure; all the ingenuity of the world must devise new pleasures for him, because only in the moment of pleasure does he find rest...' (E/O, 2:186).

Judge William concludes that every aesthete, from the fortune-seeker to the frantic voluptuary, has failed to achieve a stable self: either the source of pleasure is transient (physical beauty) or provided 'externally' (talent), or a person is simply lost in a wash of ever-shifting desires, each one fading as it is satisfied. As Judge William points out (and as we saw in the First Movement) everyone seeks a meaning for their lives, one that needs to be materially realized, and that meaning is, of course, what structures a narrative for that life over time. The redoubtable Anti-Climacus describes the formation of a self as a challenge every human being must confront;[4] the opposed dimensions of the human constitution, the 'finite and the infinite', the 'temporal and the eternal', and 'freedom and necessity' pose questions that demand answers: Who are you? How do you spend your time, and why? What is of infinite worth to you, and how does that value show up in your daily existence?

The aesthetes have failed to answer these questions in a way that provides them with a stable identity and enduring significance. All of the aesthetes are thus in despair, meaning that they have failed to commit themselves to an enterprise that coherently satisfies the opposed demands of being human. Anti-Climacus claims that the 'sickness unto death' is in fact despair: '... accordingly, it can take three forms: in despair not to be conscious of having a self (not despair in the strict sense); in despair not to will to be oneself; in despair to will to be oneself' (SUD, 13). This final, and highest, form of despair draws close to the solution, but not quite. The answer to the dilemma of despair is, as we saw in the First Movement, found when a person makes an absolute commitment to his or her vocation in the presence of God: 'The formula that describes the state of the self when despair is completely rooted out is this: in relating itself to itself and in willing to be itself, the self rests transparently in the relation to the power that established it' (SUD, 14).

The aesthetes, of course, have not committed themselves to a unique, singular vocation—one that must be realized individually—but to their *capacity* to have pleasure. This commitment has failed to resolve the constitutional despair of being human; all their pleasure-chasing has merely staved off the day of reckoning. The aesthetes have failed to become themselves, but only A, argues Judge William, has

[4] Or indeed fail to see that there is a constitutional problem in being human in the first place: this is the first and most common form of what Anti-Climacus calls '... not despair in the strict sense' (SUD, 13).

pushed the issue to breaking point; his despair is of the highest and most instructive kind. As the Judge remarks,

> But there is a difference between despair and despair. If I imagine an artist, for example a painter who goes blind, he perhaps—unless there is something more profound in him—will despair. He despairs over this particular matter, and if his sight is restored again, the despair would terminate. This is not the case with you . . . your soul is too profound for this to happen to you. In an external sense this has not happened to you either. You still have in your power all the elements for an aesthetic life-view. You have financial means, independence; your health is undiminished; your mind is still vigorous; and you have never been unhappy because a young girl would not love you. And yet you are in despair. (E/O, 2:194)

Here Judge William presents A as a 'best case scenario' for the aesthetic life: A, although dependent, like all aesthetes, on various external conditions, still has many riches to enjoy—wealth, bodily vigor, an imaginative sensitivity that is immune to a young girl's tears. Who could be better positioned for at least the attempt to live solely for pleasure? But A has worked through all the possible iterations of the aesthetic; he realizes that it cannot deliver on its shiny promises. The artist relying on his talent despairs if he loses his eyesight, because his pleasure-device, painting, is thwarted; A understands that pleasure itself, when placed at the center of a person's life, *will be thwarted regardless.* Judge William concludes, 'Your thought has rushed ahead; you have seen through the vanity of everything, but you have not gone further' (E/O, 2:194).

The 'Choice-Constituted' Self

What is A to do? 'You hover above yourself', the Judge admonishes (E/O, 2:199); '. . . you are always afraid of continuity, chiefly because it deprives you of the chance to delude yourself' (E/O, 2:198). Of course, a continuously meaningful existence is what A set out to secure for himself, and now, to borrow Judge William's famous slogan, A must 'choose his despair': 'Choose despair, then, because despair itself is a choice . . . And in despairing a person chooses again, and what then does he choose? He chooses himself, not in his immediacy, not as this accidental individual, but he chooses himself in his eternal validity' (E/O, 2:211). A, with his infernal, tricksy talent for shifting his attention from one reflective pursuit to another, must confront the raw fact that he is himself the source of his despair; he has *chosen* this round of imagined delights and seductions for himself. Now, if A embraces choice, he will have grasped the essence of the ethical: freedom. '... [T]he most abstract expression for this "self" that makes him who he is ... is nothing other than freedom' (E/O, 2:215).

Of course! A must see that he is constructed by his choices, and seize hold of the constitutional freedom he has as his human birthright; after all, 'freedom', according to Anti-Climacus, is indeed one of the dimensions of being human that demand to be satisfied. Many things are possible, yes: but only a choice allows something to spring into being. The Judge concludes, '... I as free spirit am born out of the principle of contradiction or am born through my choosing myself' (E/O, 2:215–16).

Let Judge William continue his triumphant peroration on choice while we pause. Why is it that a life committed to articulating and discriminating what is available for choosing, and constructing a narrative about that judgment, has an inherent existential superiority to a life that pursues enjoyment? The answer is disarmingly (and dangerously) simple: a life committed to choice is not vulnerable to accident. The aesthete operates at the mercy of the 'external condition': beauty fades, faculties wither, fortunes disappear, and the call of desire creates a trail of satiation and depletion. Choice, however, is immune to such vagaries. Even if what Judge William chooses is burdensome or ill-advised, he can always reconvene the court and hear the case one more time; he may always re-assess the evidence and choose again. Judge William has secured a robustly meaningful life, and a solid identity as a person who is who he is because of what he has chosen.

But what does the 'choice-constructed' self have to do with marriage? Why is this relationship the apotheosis of the ethical life?

Judge William takes seriously the vow that binds a married pair: he dubs marriage a '... synthesis of falling in love and resolution' (SLW, 109). Of course, the thrills of falling in love are familiar to A, but resolution—the moment when a person freely takes up a formal, civic commitment to that emotion—is what establishes a self: as Judge

William puts it, 'A person's total ideality lies first and last in resolution' (SLW, 108). The 'self' that is thus created, however, is an *ethical* one: the Judge concludes, 'The resolving is the ethical, is freedom . . . ' (SLW, 111). Marriage becomes the ideal mechanism for repairing the constitutional tension between freedom and necessity: life's ordinary, daily chores are now suffused with the significance of the absolute resolution to share that life with another person. This institution now has a kind of ontological significance: 'Marriage I regard, then, as the highest *telos* of individual life . . . ' (SLW, 101).[5]

The language of teleology is curiously suggestive of Johannes de silentio's analysis of faith in *Fear and Trembling*. In 'Problem I' de silentio begins by giving us this definition of the ethical: 'The ethical as such is the universal, and as the universal it applies to everyone, which may be expressed from another angle by saying that it is in force at every moment. It rests immanently in itself, has nothing outside itself that is its *telos*, but is itself the *telos* for everything outside itself, and when the ethical has assimilated this into itself it goes no further' (FT, 46). The 'ethical' exhausts our conceptual arsenal. All deliberation has the *telos*, or goal, of making our choices clear: the issues must be fully elaborated and the concepts being used need to be adequately defined. Beyond that—what? What could a rational agent want beyond this enterprise of clarity?

Faith, of course, is (paradoxically) precisely that which is beyond the *telos* of the ethical, that ' . . . the single individual as the particular is higher than the universal and is justified over against the latter not as subordinate but superior to it . . . ' (FT, 48).

In the Prelude we considered, briefly, the infinite resignation that is the necessary step before the life of faith. Resignation is also a kind of conceptual reckoning, an evaluation of the mortal, finite state of a person's affairs. The knight of infinite resignation uses his reason to conclude that he cannot invest his infinite passion in a finite, mortal

---

[5] We need to remember that we are working with two epistolary versions of Judge William: his initial response to A's life is *Either/Or II*, which was composed slightly earlier than *Fear and Trembling* (both published in 1843); this particular passage from *Stages On Life's Way* was published in 1845, and is thus clearly intended to be read in light of Johannes de silentio's meditation on the 'teleological suspension of the ethical'.

girl: so he gives her up, and relegates her to imagination's cupboard. He will remember her, of course, and remain committed to the *idea* of his beloved, but he will not have a relationship with the actual person. (On the other hand, the faithful knight, please remember, 'gets the girl'.)

Judge William's assertion that marriage is the *telos* of an individual's life challenges de silentio's distinction between the life of resignation and the life of faith. The Judge certainly believes that the opposed dimensions of the human frame need to be resolved by means of a commitment, but he claims that a person's resolute devotion to a self that is a *choosing self* is the answer to this existential dilemma. Evidently, the Knight of Infinite Resignation has made a mistake: rather than invest infinite worth in the idea of his beloved, he should have infinitely committed himself to the *choice* of his beloved. Now the fount of significance flows freely: the knight may plunge with zest into the myriad conventional details of married life—and invest them with infinite worth—while responding flexibly to the mishaps and even the horrors of life: should something dreadful happen to his wife, Judge William will still be able to negotiate that terrible scene with a choice-driven narrative about what, and how, this turn of events has significance for him.

Unsurprisingly, the good Judge has made a compelling case for himself. Why, then, isn't Judge William's 'ethical-erotic' response to the demands of being human the right one? What does 'faith', as described by Johannes de silentio, provide that this rich and coherent account does not?

Temporal Significance

Let us review what is admirable in the Judge's account. As we have seen, the Judge argues that marriage as an ethical resolution is the appropriate response to the synthetic tension of being human; in fact, he anticipates the words of Anti-Climacus on the constitution of the self: '... marriage is precisely that immediacy which contains mediacy, that infinity which contains finitude, that eternity which contains temporality...' (E/O, 2:94). A person who is committed to the choice of their spouse can, says the Judge, find their finite conditions, and indeed the way that they spend their time, buoyed up in a great sea of infinite value and eternal devotion (as spelled out in the public vows taken in the celebration of marriage). Judge William concludes, '[love is] sensuous and yet spiritual, but it is more, for the word "spiritual [*aandelig*]" applied to the first love is closest to meaning that it is psychical [*sjælelig*], that it is the sensuous permeated by spirit. It is freedom and necessity . . . ' (E/O, 2:60–1).

The choice to marry thus addresses the constitutional demand for a fulfilling freedom expressed in the quotidian details of life; however, the marriage-choice also attends to the most glaring deficiency of the aesthetic way of life: it makes sense of a person's *time*. Remember the temporal mess of Johannes the Seducer:[6] he thinks that his seductions provide some kind of escape from time itself into an erotically numinous eternal present: but of course they do not. Johannes' narrative of his serial seductions has only cheated him of the precious moments that actually do constitute his life, ones that are quickly and irrevocably fading away.

Marriage, avers the Judge, is a resolution made in the face of absolute temporal limits. A person must resolve to take a wife or a husband, and that choice does not have the luxury of infinite time: 'To fritter life away looking for the ideal (as if all such seeking were anything but stupidity and presumption) without understanding the meaning of either erotic love or marriage, without ever understanding the innocent enthusiasm that jestingly reminds youth that time is passing, that time is passing—this is an existence devoid of ideas' (SLW, 107). The aesthete, always absorbed in reflective anticipation, is never aware that at every moment his refusal to choose is destroying the possibility of establishing a self through the choice of a mate. The Judge admonishes A at the beginning of *Either/Or II*: 'But you do lose; you lose your time . . . ' (E/O, 2:11), and time, once spent, cannot be retrieved, despite all the cunning gambits of recollection. As the Judge

[6] Judge William specifically addresses the Seducer's tactics in *Either/Or II*: he remarks, 'Even if [love] can never be repeated like the first time, do you think that there would still be a tolerable way of escape, that one would be rejuvenated by experiencing the illusion in others, so that one would enjoy the infinity and novelty in the originality of the individual whose virginal girdle of illusion was not as yet undone? Such things betray just as much desperation as corruption . . . ' (E/O, 2:127).

bluntly puts it: 'Well, this is indeed the meaning of time, and it is the fate of humankind and of individuals to live in it' (E/O, 2:128).[7]

So: what's wrong with Judge William's account, and why is this stage of life (somehow) less than the life of faith? To once again quote Johannes de silentio's crucial remark about the life of faith in *Fear and Trembling*, '*Timeligheden, Endeligheden er det, hvorom Alt dreier sig*'—'Temporality, finitude, is what it is all about': surely the Judge is giving voice to this claim?

The distinction between the ethical life and the life of faith is initially difficult to make. Notice the 'faithful' way in which Judge William characterizes marriage: 'The genuinely idealizing resolution must be just as concrete as it is abstract ... there is nothing between heaven and earth so concrete as a marriage and the marital relationship, nothing so inexhaustible; even the most insignificant thing has its significance, and while the marriage commitment flexibly spans a lifetime ... it encircles the moment, and every moment, just as flexibly' (SLW, 114). Furthermore, says the Judge, 'What life is happier than his for whom everything has meaning; how could life become long for the person to whom the moment has meaning?' (SLW, 115).

Our (silent) tax collector, were he to speak, could not express his own faithful condition any better. Judge William even makes use of a version of 'epistemic flexibility', the endless resourcefulness of the marital condition, infinitely so, even as it is necessarily realized in utterly specific, finite situations. The Judge's life is filled with meaningful abundance, just as it is for the faithful tax collector.

Curiously, Judge William also appropriates the notion of *Dobbelt-Bevægelse*, the 'double movement' that is the hallmark of the life of faith. (Recall that Johannes the Seducer made use of the 'double movement' in describing what will happen to Cordelia as the seduction proceeds.) The Judge gives this explanation: ' ... in his life, every person goes through the double movement—first, if I may put it this way, the pagan movement, where erotic love belongs, and then the Christian movement, whose expression is marriage ... ' (E/O, 2:36). The Judge's double movement is very different from the Seducer's: rather than moving from an idealized conception of a lover to the quotidian

[7] See also E/O, 2:118, 2:136, and 2:138.

reality of the person himself (and thus understanding the former as realized in the latter), the Judge conceives of this movement as an initial, immediate passion that moves to the grounded, resolute daily life of a marriage. (Clearly, both of these differ from Johannes de silentio's understanding of the 'double movement' of faith, which takes a person from the resignation of conceptual clarity to a life lived in the face of finitude's incontrovertible limits.)

Finally, Judge William makes a declaration about his faith: '... there is only one attribute that makes [a married man] loveable, and that is faith, absolute faith in marriage' (SLW, 91). He claims that he has 'the honor of fighting under the victorious banner of the happy first love alongside her through whom I feel the meaning of my life ... ' (SLW, 93). How is Judge William's faithful married condition different from the knight of faith who 'gets the girl'? (FT, 39).

Judge William's rendition of the 'marital-ethical' certainly *sounds* like the life of faith. Let's return for a moment to the Judge's claim that marriage is the *telos* of an individual's life: we have already noted Johannes de silentio's claim that faith is—paradoxically—'higher' than the ethical, and that the faithful life is lived in a 'teleological suspension of the ethical': the individual self, acting in faith, lives in such a way that the end, or *telos*, of the ethical is suspended (FT, 49). The goal of the ethical, of course, is to be understood, and a person acting ethically is always obliged to be able to give reasons for her actions: why this choice, and not that one? Why this project, or this marriage partner, and not something altogether different? Why? An ethical person must be able to give reasons for what she does, and she must be prepared to defend those reasons (and be prepared to revisit that defense, again and again).

It is important that faith dwells in a suspension of the *telos* of the ethical, and not (as some readers of Kierkegaard occasionally suggest) an *abrogation* of the *telos* of the ethical. 'Faith' designates the way in which a fully realized self navigates the world, and not merely a set of beliefs that allow a self to so navigate: but this is not to say that faith lacks, or has overturned, the rational conclusions about the nature of things that resignation has put in place. No: as we saw in the Prelude, a faithful person must become resigned—must look the impossibility of his finite undertakings in the eye—before he can live out his projects faithfully.

The faithful individual, now resigned to the rational limits of the world, can—of course—give (some) reasons for his actions, but the activity of reason-giving is not the goal of faith: in fact, that kind of ethical activity is existentially circumscribed by the demands of the life being lived. Consider Abraham, located in the present moment as he sets out to do what his reason tells him cannot, and should not, be done: when Isaac asks where the sacrificial lamb is, Abraham is able to answer Isaac—truthfully—that God will provide the lamb for the sacrifice.

Here is Johannes de silentio's account of this moment in Genesis:

> From this one sees the double movement in Abraham's soul as previously described. If Abraham had merely resigned Isaac and done no more, then he would have uttered an untruth, for he indeed knows that God demands Isaac for a sacrifice, and he knows that he himself precisely at this moment is ready to sacrifice him. After having made this movement, he has at every moment made the next one, has made the movement of faith by virtue of the absurd. In principle, he utters no untruth, for by virtue of the absurd it is indeed possible that God could do something entirely different. He utters no untruth, then, but neither does he say anything, for he speaks in a foreign tongue. (FT, 105)

Faithful action 'speaks in a foreign tongue' because it stands in a suspended relation to the absolute goal of the ethical explanation. Even so, Abraham does answer Isaac—that much of the ethical obligation is still in place—but his answer does not make any sense, since Abraham himself knows that it is he who must wield the blade: the 'resigned' answer to Isaac would be that he himself is slated for sacrifice. But Abraham's reply is faithful: he tells the truth within the frame of the present moment, not anticipating what his reason surely tells him will inevitably follow. The *telos* of the ethical, that Abraham must use his knowledge to account for the situation at hand, is temporarily in abeyance.

Paying for the Ethical

Frater Taciturnus, at the end of *Stages on Life's Way*, deftly sums up the demands of the ethical: '... the ethical [is] the sphere of requirement (and this requirement is so infinite that the individual always goes bankrupt)... the ethical is a passageway—which one nevertheless does not pass through once and for all...' (SLW, 477).

Both of these tropes are instructive. A person committed to the ethical life will necessarily go 'bankrupt': after all, when will the reckoning end? We have already observed that the ethical sphere requires explanations: why this choice, and not that one? The good Judge is fond of this kind of choice-narrative, but perhaps his prolixity is covering up a dwindling fund. Judge William will never be done explaining, because he has never committed himself to something, or someone, in the world; instead, he is committed to the *choice* of something, or someone. The significance of his choice lies in the choosing, and not in the absolute worth of that which is chosen. Thus Judge William announces to A: 'What takes precedence in my Either/Or is, then, the ethical. Therefore, the point is still not that of choosing something; the point is not the reality of that which is chosen but *the reality of choosing*' (E/O, 2:176, emphasis mine). Recall his locution in describing his marriage: his wife is '... [she] through whom I feel the meaning of my life...' (SLW, 93): His *wife* is not the meaning of his life: she is merely the locus for the meaningfulness of his marital choice. In describing the existential content of his marriage, Judge William successfully mimics the Knight of Faith's ability to dwell joyfully with his beloved, even as, at every moment, the sword hangs over her head (FT, 43): the Judge remarks, 'A married man risks every day, and every day the sword of duty hangs over his head, and the journal is kept up as long as the marriage keeps on, and the ledger of responsibility is never closed...' (SLW, 117). The sword here is not emblematic of the dangers of mortal life, but of the potential failure to carry on the account of his marriage; the 'ledger' is never closed because the Judge will never finish justifying—and elaborating on that justification—the wife, and indeed the life, that he has chosen.

The second trope of Frater Taciturnus, of the ethical sphere as a 'passageway', indicates a deeper problem: in a sense, the Judge can never really get started with his ethical reckoning. Even the choice to marry, let alone the person to whom he binds himself, is in need of constant explanatory vigilance and prolix care. This is why a person in the ethical stage of life can never 'pass through' it: the narrative that bears up and makes sense of a person's choices is an ongoing task for that person.

We have already seen why a life committed to choice is preferable to a life focused on obtaining pleasure: the ethical life is not vulnerable to accident; even if a particular choice goes badly, the ethical agent has not lost that which makes his life coherent and meaningful: that person is still a reflective chooser. But the drawback to this life is equally clear: when choice is 'world-defining' it is impossible to have any standards for making particular choices, since these standards too must be chosen: hence the endless explanatory round begins.

What, then, is the difference between the ethical Judge William, and a version that we may well imagine, a *faithful* Judge William—one who has achieved selfhood and who thus dwells in faith, as our cheerful tax collector does?

Clearly, Judge William believes that he is an established self: here is his earnest description of what he calls 'the moment of choice':

> When around one everything has become silent, solemn as a clear, starlit night, when the soul comes to be alone in the whole world, then before one there appears . . . the eternal power itself, then the heavens seem to open, and the I chooses itself or, more correctly, receives itself . . . then the personality receives the accolade of knighthood that ennobles it for an eternity. He does not become someone other than he was before, but he becomes himself . . . greatness is not to be this or that but to be oneself, and every human being can be this if he so wills it. (E/O, 2:177)

Notice that Judge William helps himself to the language of 'knighthood': at every moment the Judge is freely making specific, finite choices that he can invest with absolute worth, an undertaking that surely resembles the knight of faith's absorption in the finite. But it is also clear that Judge William finds his choices meaningful in his *expression* of them. Here is how he describes the transition from falling in love to marriage:

> . . . falling in love is nature's most profound myth . . . but the *resolution* is the triumphant victor . . . *the resolution is the true form of love, the true explanation and transfiguration*; therefore marriage is sacred and blessed by God. It is civic, for by marriage the lovers belong to the state and the fatherland and the common concerns of their fellow citizens. It is poetic, inexpressibly so, just as is falling in love, but the resolution is the conscientious translator that translates the enthusiasm into actuality, and this translator is so scrupulous, oh, so scrupulous! (SLW, 117, emphasis mine)

The sanctity of the marriage flows not from the inarticulate, immediate passion of the lovers, but from the 'resolution' of publicly expressed vows. The conceptual commitment that structures the married estate is its meaning, not the utterly particular relations of the two people involved. The 'conscientious translation' is the ongoing activity of articulating those vows of fidelity, of emotional and material support, and the value of the marriage is to be found in that serial declamation.

This dependence on conceptual expression is precisely the test and 'temptation' that the Knight of Faith avoids. As Johannes de silentio tells us, '... this knight knows that it is glorious to belong to the universal. He knows that it is beautiful and beneficial to be the particular individual who translates himself into the universal, one who, so to speak, personally produces a clean-cut, elegant, and insofar as possible flawless edition of himself, readable by all ... But he knows as well that higher than this there winds a lonely trail ... he knows that it is frightful to be born outside the universal ... ' And, speaking specifically of Abraham, Johannes concludes, '... he accomplishes nothing for the universal but is himself only being tried and tested' (FT, 66–7). The knight of faith cannot 'accomplish' anything for the universal—that is, for the conceptual realm—because the absolute particularity of the knight's vocation outstrips what can be captured in language.[8] This is not to say that the knight of faith cannot speak: as we saw, Abraham does answer Isaac's question, and does so truthfully, but his answer only expresses the absurd unfolding of Abraham's absolute commitment to his son as a gift from God as he continues on the path to Mount Moriah.

Judge William's 'faith' in his married condition is a commitment to his powers of articulation. This is quite different from the knight of faith who 'gets the girl' (FT, 39); in a sense, Judge William gets no one at all, but rather an *account* of who he is as he lives out his marital vows and obligations.

The ethical 'self' that Judge William has established has turned out to be—in a very different way—as unsustainable as the aesthetic 'self'. His commitment to the life of choice in general, and to marriage in

---

[8] The difference between the 'objective' and 'subjective' elements in faithful action will be discussed in the Postlude.

particular, is a commitment to rendering himself via 'universals'. Judge William's life as a chooser does not pick him out as an individual: as he puts it, ' . . . in the resolution he will, through the universal, place himself in a relationship with God. He does not dare to cling to himself as a singular individual . . . His comfort is precisely that he is just like other human beings and in this common humanity is in relationship with God . . . ' (SLW, 164). Of course, the overarching directive of Kierkegaard's religious corpus is that one is called to become 'that single individual' before God, and certainly not one who is in some sense 'mediated' by the presence of other persons. Judge William gives himself away when he remarks, 'A religiously developed person makes a practice of referring everything to God, of permeating and saturating every finite relation with *the thought of God* and thereby consecrating and ennobling it' (E/O, 2:43, emphasis mine). Certainly, the tax collector's cheerful, focused existence (or indeed Abraham's terrible, certain majesty as he makes his way to Mount Moriah) does not owe its faithful quality to a *thought* about God.

Judge William's remarks about a person's vocation (inadvertently) make clear the way in which the ethical life invites the 'leveling' we discussed in the First Movement. He chides A for preferring 'talent' to 'duty' when it comes to thinking about his work in the world. A, of course, aims at turning every occupation into a pleasure-device; Judge William imagines the kind of advice an aesthete might give about a person's employment: 'One's work nevertheless ought not to be work in the strict sense but should be able to be continually defined as pleasure. A person should discover some aristocratic talent in himself that distinguishes him from the crowd . . . Life then has a new meaning for him, since he has his work, a work that nevertheless is really his pleasure' (E/O, 2:290). If a person lacks such a defining talent, so much the worse for him; of course, even those fortunate, talented few will fail to be pleased by their craft all of the time. Judge William's objection is deeper: to treat human talent as a means for pleasure is to misunderstand the kind of work that talent should provide, and indeed the work that every person ought to do. Here is his account of the ethicist's retort:

> 'It is every human being's duty to have a calling'. More he cannot say, because the ethical as such is always abstract, and there is no abstract calling for all human beings. On the contrary, he presupposes that each

person has a particular calling. Which calling our hero should choose, the ethicist cannot tell him, because for that a detailed knowledge of the aesthetic aspects of his whole personality is required, and even if the ethicist did have this knowledge, he would still refrain from choosing for him, because in that case he would indeed deny his own life-view. What the ethicist can tell him is that there is a calling for every human being and, when our hero has found his, he is to choose it ethically. (E/O, 2:291–2)

Here Judge William draws very close to Anti-Climacus's analysis of the forging of a self, in God's presence, through a life-commitment. He goes on to point out that 'When a person has a calling, he generally has a norm outside of himself, which, without making him a slave, nevertheless gives him some indication of what he has to do, maps out his time for him, often provides him with the occasion to begin' (E/O, 2:294). Here we have the crucial elements for addressing the human condition: a person must satisfy both dimensions of human experience; the yearning for infinite worth and eternal significance has to be rendered materially, even as the clock metes out a measure and the day fades. A person who follows her vocation will find herself meaningfully reflected even in the humblest chores, since that work is illuminated by its inherent purpose.

But notice: Judge William asserts that a person must *choose* his calling. This claim is obviously in keeping with his commitment to the life of choice, but it once again underscores the ontologically desperate nature of the ethical life. A person chooses her life's work: but how? People are endlessly inventive and capable, and many kinds of work are available to everyone: should a person wait tables? Write philosophy books? Walk dogs, drive a taxi, become a pharmacist? A drug dealer? How does a person judge what is best to do? Then, having chosen, a person is, of course, obliged to give reasons for that choice, and it is that reason-giving activity that never comes to an end; this is the 'ethical passageway' so aptly described by Frater Taciturnus. The job of the ethicist is to provide a trim, fully annotated life-narrative, yet his audience will always clamor for more. Our fellow humans are never tired of asking and answering questions, and of framing, and re-framing, those replies. Judge William remarks:

[a person] discovers that the self he chooses has a boundless multiplicity within itself inasmuch as it has a history, a history in which he

acknowledges identity with himself... in this history he stands in relation to other individuals in the race and to the whole race, and... yet
he is the person he is only through this history. This is why it takes
courage to choose oneself, for at the same time as he seems to be
isolating himself most radically he is most radically sinking himself
into the root by which he is bound up with the whole. (E/O, 2:216)

Indeed: the ethicist is doomed to give an account of his work, his life, his
choices, and that chronicle of self-reckoning can never come to an end.
Judge William's peroration to A now has the sound of someone constitutionally averse to a silence that reveals its own narrative plight. Judge
William is condemned to choose (the specter of Sartre enters the scene),
and the meaningfulness of those choices can only be located in the
reasons he chooses to assemble for those choices, ad infinitum.

Judge William is an admirable character, and his behavior does, in
some ways, resemble that of our tax collector. As we have seen, the
Judge is exuberant (indeed, erotically so); he is passionately focused on
his work in the world, and confident about the significance of what he
does. The Judge also gives voice to some of the features of faith
described by both Anti-Climacus and Johannes de silentio: Judge
William understands that a meaningful life is the constitutional birthright of every person, and that everyone is thus obliged to get about
the business of finding, and dwelling in, her or his unique vocation.

And yet: some of the Judge's criticisms of A are also all-too-familiar
reminders of the Judge's own deliberative behavior. When Judge William tells A that '... the finite cannot survive in your thought' and that
A is, in Judge William's estimation,'... finished with the finite altogether
...' (E/O, 2:202), the Judge's wife comes to mind: where is *she*, the
enfleshed, breathing, aging woman, in all of the Judge's life-choices? Is
Judge William really invested in the finite? Perhaps this lacuna is why,
even after many pages dedicated to praising his marriage (and even after,
in *Stages on Life's Way*, the editor Victor Eremita has treated the reader to a
sweet vignette of the Judge and his wife, having tea together), the Judge's
wife remains unnamed. Since her significance lies in Judge William's (no
doubt admirable) choice of her, she can really only ever reflect the sound
substance of his judgment. She is 'wife-placeholder', and nothing more.[9]

---

[9] Judge William admits that he doesn't even know what she looks like (SLW, 125).

'Always in the Wrong'

The sermon that Judge William sends on to A (and that serves as the
coda for the second volume of *Either/Or*) provides some important
hints about what has gone wrong in the ethical sphere, and what the
next attempt at selfhood will look like. The 'Ultimatum' of *Either/Or*
is a copy of a sermon written by a long-standing friend of Judge
William's, a pastor tending to a parish not in fashionable Copenhagen, but out on the rugged heath of Jylland, a congregation of
peasant farmers and their families. Judge William gives A an elaborate
description of this homespun pastor (a person who is clearly out of
keeping with the refined tastes of A the aesthete): 'He was a stocky little
fellow, lively, cheerful, and unusually jovial. Although in the depths of
his soul he was deeply earnest, in his outward life he seemed to follow
the advice "Let things take their course." Scholarly studies enthralled
him, but he was no good at taking examinations... He possessed,
among his external qualities, a stentorian voice; among his intellec-
tual-spiritual qualities, he had an originality that always distinguished
him in the little circle in which I learned to know him' (E/O, 2:337–8).

The Jylland pastor's resemblance to our tax collector is irresistible.
The tax collector is, of course, also constituted by a lively joy in all
things; he too enjoys using his voice (in the tax collector's case, to sing
hymns loudly with 'a good pair of lungs' (FT, 33)). The pastor
certainly follows the tax collector's model of 'letting things take their
course': as Johannes de silentio puts it, the tax collector '... lets things
take their course with a freedom from care as if he were a reckless
good-for-nothing and yet buys every moment he lives at the opportune time for the dearest price, for he does not do even the slightest
thing except by virtue of the absurd' (FT, 33). The tax collector's
faithful way of being in the world is clearly much more than a 'letting-
go', but some kind of disciplined 'attending-to'. The pastor has evidently appropriated this ability to dwell mindfully in the present
moment—whatever that might mean.

Of course, this problem has dogged us from the beginning of our
investigation: how does the tax collector, our putative, imagined
Knight of Faith, do what he does? Thus far we have been confined
to observing—as Johannes de silentio does, as he conjures him—the
comportment of the tax collector, and the success with which he

navigates his environment. The images of the tax collector are intriguing and compelling, but utterly silent. We cannot learn anything by merely watching him.

Judge William's account of his pastor-friend, however, is equipped with a bit more information about his interior life. Judge William tells A that the pastor was initially unhappy with his post on the heath, ministering to a peasant flock: '... he thought his work was too insignificant for him. But now he has regained his contentment ... "The heath in Jylland", he says, "is a real playground for me, a private study room beyond compare. I go out there on Saturday and meditate on my sermons, and everything unfolds for me ... *I achieve total absorption in myself*"' (E/O, 2:338, emphasis mine). Like the (chimerical) comprehensively satiated Don Giovanni—as well as the ever-rapt cheer of the tax collector—the pastor has achieved a wholeness of self that generates his focused pleasure in his work. Surely the pastor's sermon will provide an insight about what it is that orients this behavior.

And indeed it does. The sermon is titled 'The Upbuilding That Lies in the Thought That in Relation to God we are Always in the Wrong'. Here we move decisively to a religious account of the self, one that— to return to the wisdom of Frater Taciturnus—is '... the sphere of fulfillment, but, please note, not fulfillment such as when one fills an alms box or a sack with gold, for repentance has specifically created a boundless space and as a consequence the religious contradiction: simultaneously to be out on 70,000 fathoms of water and yet be joyful' (SLW, 476–7).

Repentance is a theme that Judge William briefly treats in his letter to A.[10] In thinking about the various kinds of love that a person experiences—love of parents, of wife—the love of God requires a singular mode of expression: '... it is "repentance." If I do not love him in this way, then I do not love him absolutely, out of my innermost being ... as soon as I love freely and love God, then I repent' (E/O, 2: 216). Judge William, however, does not pursue this line of thinking; he remarks that since he is writing as a layman he will leave the

---

[10] In fact, it follows his thoughts about how an ethically faithful person stands in relation to the rest of the ethical community.

subsequent observations to the theologians (E/O, 2:218). This tacit
admission of the limits of the ethical point of view—an admirable
silence on the Judge's part—anticipates this textual moment when the
pastor will have his say.[11]

In order to understand the kind of repentance that accompanies the
religious life, we need to consider the claim that 'in relation to God we
are always in the wrong', and how this thought is an 'upbuilding' one.
The pastor's sermon begins with a prayer of thanksgiving and confession (of always being in the wrong in relation to God); he then
provides the Gospel reading, Luke 19:41–4, in which Jesus sorrowfully
meditates on the catastrophe that will befall Jerusalem. The pastor
then asks the perennially difficult question about those who suffered as
Jerusalem was destroyed: 'Must the righteous, then suffer with the
unrighteous?' (E/O, 2:342). The pastor rejects as 'cowardly and
dismal' the thought that such things happened long ago, and that
now we live in prosperity: *that* such things have happened is grievous
and alarming enough. A person might, suggests the pastor, be weighed
down with this thought; even when struggling to achieve justice, a
person may well conclude that '... it would be unreasonable of God
to require the impossible of him. One does what one can' (E/O, 2:345).

Does this thought, that a person only does 'what one can', provide
comfort? The pastor asserts that it does not: 'Was it such an easy
matter for you, my listener, to determine how much that is: what one
can? ... Was not the real reason for your unrest that you did not know
for sure how much one can do, that it seems to you to be so infinitely
much at one moment, and at the next moment so very little?' (E/O,
2:345).

Here we have returned to the message (as rendered by Kierkegaard) of James 1:17–22: 'Every gift is good and perfect'. (Recall that
one of Kierkegaard's discourses on this verse, titled 'Every Good and
Every Perfect Gift', was published in May of 1843, just three months
after the publication of *Either/Or*.) As we saw in the First Movement,
Kierkegaard interprets this passage epistemologically: we are not in a
position—God's position—to judge the absolute scope and nature of

---

[11] David Law provides a careful analysis of the way in which the 'Ultimatum'
serves as a transition to the religious authorship (1996: 233–59).

what befalls us. A person dwelling in faith will 'take up' life's events and accidents as 'good and perfect'—an orientation that does not proclaim that a particular misfortune is in fact good; rather, that person lives (paradoxically) with the assurance that nothing, no situation, is beyond God's transformational power.

The Jylland pastor's sermon certainly anticipates the two discourses on James 1:17–22 when he asks the question: what will truly calm a person, when she or he reflects on the suffering of the innocent?[12] The pastor argues that calm is achieved when a person meditates on the notion that the *upbuilding* lies in the thought that in relation to God we are always in the wrong (E/O, 2:346). He carefully takes his listener through an analysis of what this homily might mean: surely it is most painful to realize that one is in the wrong, and—surely—a person wants to rectify this condition, to return to 'being in the right'. The pastor imagines a typical kind of quotidian harm: 'Your life brings you into a multiplicity of relationships with other people. Some of them love justice and righteousness; others do not seem to want to practice them—they do you a wrong . . . However much they outrage me, you say, they will not be able to deprive me of this peace—that I know I am right and that I suffer wrong' (E/O, 2:347). Judge William comes to mind: the Judge is a person who strives to determine who has been wronged, and the ways in which his assessment is in fact the correct one. But the question, says the pastor, is not whether a person is right (and satisfyingly so: the pastor remarks that to be in the right is a ' . . . joy that presumably everyone has tasted . . . ' (E/O, 2:347)): the question is whether this position of self-satisfied rectitude is the thought that will 'upbuild' a person (and hence replace anxiety with calm). It is not, says the pastor, because a person's certainty that he is right bars him or her from the infinite capacity that attends a love-relationship. When a person is wronged by a loved one, it is hardly the case that being in the right is *comforting* (or indeed edifying); instead, that person wants to find a way to 'speak in his defense' and cast himself in the position of the wrongdoer.

The pastor presents us with a compelling psychological portrait. We are no doubt happy to praise ourselves for seeing, and doing, what

---

[12] More on this topic in the Postlude.

is best, and the desire to castigate our fellow creatures for their inferior judgment is certainly all-too-human. But such a position, says the pastor, is closed off from love's possibilities: a lover never admits of impediments; a person who loves will always prefer to be in the wrong.

Here is the pastor's explanation:

> It is painful, then, to be in the wrong; . . . [but] it is upbuilding to be in the wrong . . . This is indeed a contradiction! How can this be explained except by saying that in the one case you are forced to acknowledge what in the second case you wish to acknowledge? . . . How can this be explained except by saying that in the one case you loved, in the other you did not—in other words, in the one case you were in an infinite relationship with a person, in the other case a finite relationship? Therefore, wishing to be in the wrong is an expression of an infinite relationship, and wanting to be in the right, or finding it painful to be in the wrong, is an expression of a finite relationship! Hence it is upbuilding always to be in the wrong—because *only the infinite builds up; the finite does not!* (E/O, 2:348, emphasis mine)

There are several revealing details here. In the case imagined by the pastor, a person who loves the wrongdoer shifts the perspective: the question of who is right is put aside for other, more pressing concerns: why did the wrongdoer stray? What could the wronged person have done to help the perpetrator, to save him from his own misdeeds? 'Ah, if you loved him . . . you would investigate everything . . . you would try to find something that could speak in his defense . . . if you were assigned the responsibility for this person's welfare, you would do everything that was in your power and when the other person nevertheless paid no attention to it and only caused you trouble . . . you would strive to build yourself up with the thought that you were in the wrong' (E/O, 2:348). The lover is interested *not* in being right, but in loving the other person; that desire becomes resourceful in finding ways to lovingly aid the wrongdoer.[13]

A person who adopts the position of being in the wrong is 'upbuilt' by being opened up to infinite possibilities for reframing the situation, and for seeing the behavior of those involved in a new way. Here, in thinking about what constitutes these 'infinite' possibilities (and their

---

[13] Cf. Poros and Penia from the *Symposium*; more of these two in the Coda.

impact on the 'finite'), we see a distinct and crucial shift from the
ethical point of view to the religious. Consider: for Judge William, a
person is obliged to discern, uphold and enforce the order imposed by
'universals'; our finite circumstances are meant to be understood in
light of these conceptual designations. Of course, the value of a
particular moment of finitude is measured by these infinitely valuable
concepts, and thus the finite seems to slip away (witness the vanishing
wife of the Judge: her presence is understood in terms of the conceptual place she occupies).

The Jylland pastor offers us a very different understanding of the
'infinite' and the 'finite'. Judge William, in his stern evaluation and
judgment of the world around him, renders it 'finite' in an ultimately
sterile manner: having chosen an account of how things are (and
having marshaled a set of reasoned arguments for that account), the
Judge has closed off that world-account from any further development. He has passed judgment, and the sentence will be carried out
(until, of course, he sees fit to revisit it). It is this ethical version of
finitude that the pastor is objecting to: if a person is in the right, and
certain of his or her rectitude, then that person is really done with that
situation altogether. A person who loves the wrongdoer, however, is
ready to reconsider what has happened; that person prefers to be in
the wrong rather than cast the beloved as such, and—in so doing—
make new evaluations available. The ethical person wants to get it
right; the religious person wants humbly to be in the wrong.[14] Of
course, as we saw in the case of Judge William, 'getting it right' is a
process that never ends, since the task of giving reasons is never over;
every articulation of what is the case, and why it is so, begs for further
elaboration. The pastor, in asserting that the thought of being always
in the wrong is 'upbuilding', is acknowledging these limits of human
knowledge. Every ethical claim runs headlong into this epistemic
boundary: a person can never be certain that her choices—or her
evaluation of those choices, or of the choices of others—are absolutely
the right ones.

---

[14] As C. Stephen Evans succinctly puts it, 'The religious sphere begins when an
individual acquires a sense that the demands of the ethical life are ones that cannot
possibly be fulfilled' (2004: 49).

Of course, the ethicist may well retort that 'absolute' certainty is not what ethical praxis aims at. But we have now moved beyond the purview of ethical action. To say that human knowledge is 'limited' is, of course, to anticipate the pastor's final question: what is the relation of an individual to God? The pastor thus moves swiftly from describing a human relationship to a human–divine one: if a person is willing to be in the wrong for a loved one, surely this same desire is profoundly present when a person thinks about a relationship with God. As the pastor puts it: 'Therefore this, that in relation to God you are always in the wrong, is not a truth you must acknowledge, not a consolation that alleviates your pain, not a compensation for something better, but it is *a joy in which you win a victory over yourself and over the world*, your delight, your song of praise, your adoration . . . ' (E/O, 2:351, emphasis mine). The pastor's expression anticipates Kierkegaard's own account in the three *Upbuilding Discourses* devoted to the verse from James:

> . . . certitude . . . was denied you. But then, when the busy thoughts had worked themselves weary . . . perhaps then your being grew more calm, perhaps your mind . . . developed in itself the meekness that is receptive to the word that was implanted in your soul, the word that all good and perfect gifts come from above. Then no doubt you confessed in all humility that God surely did not deceive you when he accepted your earthly wishes and foolish desires, exchanged them for you and instead gave you divine comfort and holy thoughts; that he did not treat you unfairly when he denied you a wish but in compensation created this faith in your heart, when instead of a wish, which, even if it would bring everything, at most was able to give you the whole world, *he gave you a faith by which you won God and overcame the whole world*. (EUD, 36, emphasis mine)

Setting aside for the moment what it means to 'have victory over' or to 'overcome' the world—surely we are meant to be *in* the world, just as the radiant tax collector is—the epistemic message is clear. Human knowledge-claims are perfectly necessary and serviceable (and in constant need of vigilant tending, the good Judge might add), but they are nothing in comparison to God's perfect knowledge. Human beings are frail and partial in their ability to know that their choices are the right ones, and they are therefore called to embrace their own limits, and to offer this human fallibility to God as being 'always in the wrong'.

This humble submission, however, is, importantly, *not* a defeated recognition of human imperfection. The pastor makes this decisive announcement: 'There is nothing upbuilding in acknowledging that God is always in the right, and consequently nothing upbuilding in any thought that necessarily follows from it. When you acknowledge that God is always in the right, you stand outside God, and likewise when, as a conclusion from that, you acknowledge that you are always in the wrong' (E/O, 2:350). A rational sizing-up of the existential situation only puts the penitent outside of the arena of God's loving concern. Of course humans are fallible and frail; of course they are as nothing when compared to God.

This is not the thought that the pastor urges his parishioners to have; in fact, he seems to endorse a position that stands beyond these kinds of ethical calculations. The pastor concludes, 'But when you do not claim and are not convinced by virtue of any previous acknow-ledgment that you are always in the wrong, then you are hidden in God. This is your adoration, your devotion, your piety' (E/O, 2:350). Each person, claims the pastor, is *not* meant to measure him or herself against God's perfection; instead, each is called to embody her or his own limitations in a way that 'hides them in God', or, perhaps, enfolds them in infinite possibility even as they paradoxically seize hold of their own very human limits.

But what can all of this mean? How can a person accept that she is 'always in the wrong in relation to God' without having a comparative thought about her own inadequacy and insignificance?

The Judge's choice of the Jutland pastor's trenchant sermon now appears ironically apt. The Judge is ever vigilant about his distinctions and decisions, but try as he might—or so the pastor would have it—he must always be in the wrong in relation to God. This structural impossibility of the ethical sphere, that a full accounting is never (and can never be) done, is borne out by the pastor's observation about *how* a person is meant to come to this relation to God, that is, *not* by giving any kind of account.

We now leave the highly organized realm of the ethical and move forward into an examination of the religious sphere of existence. The interior life of our faithful tax collector will finally bear some analysis, and perhaps be put to the test.

5

Fourth Movement

Tax Collector v. Tax Collector

Sin and Faith

There is a problem at the heart of this investigation, and we have been putting off the day of reckoning. Now, as our good tax collector must do, we will tot up the ledger, balance the books. The triumphant satisfaction of the tax collector, so described, draws very near to, as Johannes de silentio remarks, 'bourgeois philistinism' (FT, 32). A mere description of his sublimely cheerful *demeanor* cannot reveal how he lives his life of faith. What about the 'steps' a person must take in order to achieve faith? (Indeed, what are those 'steps'?) What about the necessary moments that mark the life of the faithful person such as the confession of sin, or communion?

Certainly, sin is one of the topics that Johannes de silentio is resolutely silent about. Only one tantalizing passage in *Fear and Trembling* brings this notion into his meditation; in a footnote Johannes remarks, '. . . I have deliberately avoided any reference to the question of sin and its reality. The whole work is aimed at Abraham and him I can still reach through immediate categories, that is, insofar as I can understand him. As soon as sin is introduced, ethics runs aground precisely upon repentance, for repentance is the highest ethical expression but precisely as such the deepest ethical self-contradiction' (FT, 86). As we saw in the Jylland pastor's sermon, repentance (of a very specific sort) is essential to the religious life; actual repentance claims the 'upbuilding' notion that 'in relation to God we are always in the wrong'. 'Repentance' is a way of orienting the self: rather than searching for conceptual (and spiritual) rectitude, the repentant sinner is infinitely concerned with the limits and failures of the human frame.

A person in the ethical sphere of existence wants to get it right; the person who dwells in the religious sphere (or, as Johannes Climacus calls it, 'Religiousness A'[1]) is infinitely aware that 'getting it right' is an impossibility.

So: ethical transgressions require better thinking, better arguments and conclusions, and a new narrative about how best to live. A person may err, but that fault is the result of flawed reasoning and inappropriate choices; Judge William's insistent pleas to A about reconsidering his own utterly disordered life-choices give voice to this very approach. The religious perspective, however, is not interested in 'better living through better thinking'; in fact, the ethical notion of 'better living' is not a part of the religious vernacular.

In order to see why this is so, we need to consider just what 'sin' is, and how it differs from the ethical category of 'doing what is wrong'.

Sin: a 'Later Immediacy'

Johannes's footnote should give us pause: how is it that repentance is both the 'highest ethical expression' and 'the deepest ethical self-contradiction'? Evidently, 'sin' speaks to a person's failure to reason clearly—and correctly—about her or his choices, but—at the same time—the category of 'sin' is ponderously greater than a failure to follow the dictates of reason.

Johannes de silentio does offer us a clue in a remark that prompts his intriguing footnote:

> Sin is not the first immediacy; *sin is a later immediacy.* In sin the single individual is already higher, in the direction of the demonic paradox, than the universal, because it is a contradiction for the universal to want to require itself of one who lacks the necessary condition. If philosophy were to imagine, among other things, that it might just cross a person's mind to want to act according to its teaching, a curious comedy could be made out of that. An ethics that ignores sin is an altogether futile discipline, but if it asserts sin, then it is for that very reason beyond itself. Philosophy teaches that the immediate should be annulled. That is true enough, but what is not true is that sin, any more than faith, is the immediate as a matter of course. (FT, 86, emphasis mine)

---

[1] See the 'First Movement'.

The category of sin, rendered as a 'later immediacy', is thus aligned with the life of faith, which is also a 'later immediacy': 'For faith is not the first immediacy but a later one. The first immediacy is the esthetic, and here the Hegelian philosophy may be right. But faith is not the esthetic or else faith has never existed because it has always existed' (FT, 72).

So: 'sin' and 'faith' are conceptually isomorphic: both of these existential conditions dwell outside of the ethical sphere in that they make an exception of themselves. This, of course, is why Johannes remarks that, if faith is understood as an expression of the aesthetic, it 'has never existed because it has always existed': faith, depicted as mere aesthetic immediacy—the squalling baby in the quest for selfhood—has always been with us, namely, as a nascent moment in the ethical development of the individual.

But faith (and, evidently, sin) outstrips ethical categories. Indeed, both faith and sin, as Johannes insists, are a 'later immediacy'.

What, then, is a 'later immediacy'?

We are certainly familiar with the notion of 'immediacy': Don Giovanni's ever-effervescent lived joy is its highest exemplar. An ongoing absorption in the current moment, unfurling with utter pleasure, is just what the aesthete wants (and our beloved tax collector actually achieves). The faithful person is indeed immersed in the world in this way, but only by means of 'infinite resignation': that is, a person dwelling in faith has made a 'double movement' from the harsh reality of finitude's limits to the infinite possibilities offered by God: ' . . . for God everything is possible' (FT, 39).

We have already encountered the 'double movement' (*Dobbelt-Bevægelse*) in both the aesthetic and ethical stages. Johannes the Seducer uses the 'double movement' as a way of describing how he will manipulate Cordelia's reaction to his wooing of her: he will enflame her with written words while being cool in her presence; she then will have to negotiate that erotic temperature difference by bringing her infinite longing to bear on her finite circumstance. (To put this strategy in a more pedestrian fashion, the Seducer is heightening Cordelia's desire by 'playing hard to get' in person.) Judge William also claims that everyone should go through what he calls a 'double movement', one in which a person transforms immediate erotic passion into the infinite resolution of marriage (E/O, 2:36).

Of course (and as we have already noted) both of these claims about a 'double movement' are very different from Johannes de silentio's account; now, however, we are in a better position to see what that difference is. The Seducer is, of course, monitoring how Cordelia *conceives* of him, and thus how she will respond to him; he anticipates that she will sit and ponder over his passionate letters in light of his behavior in person. Judge William is also pointing out a reflective strategy: even though he insists that, in marriage, erotic love is not something in the past but something present, it is nonetheless a relationship based on *resignation*: ' . . . marriage has an ethical and religious element that erotic love does not have; for this reason, marriage is based on resignation [*Resignation*] which erotic love does not have' (E/O, 2:36). The Knight of Infinite Resignation rides into view: yes, resignation is the necessary precursor to faith, but it is—according to Johannes de silentio—utterly inferior to the life of faith. As he puts it:

> Faith is preceded by a movement of infinity; only then does faith commence, unexpectedly, by virtue of the absurd. This I can well understand without therefore professing to have faith. If faith is nothing beyond what philosophy passes it off to be, then Socrates has already gone further, much further, instead of the converse, that he did not arrive at it. Intellectually, he has made the movement of . . . infinite resignation. (FT, 61)

Here we are reminded again that faith is not a thought, but a way of being in the world; it is a *phenomenon* rather than a belief. Beliefs, of course, *are* an integral part of faith's phenomenology: a person must become infinitely resigned to the world's limits, and resigned from the possibility of absolute abundance in the world, in order to seize hold of it. In other words, a faithful person has achieved ethical (that is, conceptual) mastery: she understands the limits of her circumstances and her mortal frame; she well knows that her projects, even if successful in the moment, will be lost and forgotten in the rush of human history. Indeed, the faithful person knows, and embraces, the possibility of utter failure. The faithful person is not someone who lives in a blissful dream-world: this person lives in reality, and is familiar with its every unforgiving—and temporally fleeting—contour.

Faith is thus a 'later immediacy': the life of faith is one of immediate, joyful immersion in the world ("Temporality, finitude is what it is all about' (FT, 46)), but that life has already been (to resort to Johannes's monetary trope) paid for: the person of faith understands the impossibility of human projects, but undertakes them anyway.

But what about sin, which is also (according to Johannes) a 'later immediacy'? If we follow the logic of the phenomenon of faith, we get an interesting result. Faith is founded on a person's unique vocation; when a person makes a commitment to that life-project, she must, as we just said, resign herself to its impossibility: then, of course, she simply takes up that task 'by virtue of the absurd', which turns out to be another way of saying that 'with God all things are possible' (which, the conceptually resigned person will point out, is false; all things are not possible).

Sin, therefore, must also have to do with the vocation that uniquely locates each person; that transforms a human being into 'that single individual'. If sin is also a 'second immediacy', it too must pass through some kind of conceptual stage, or a weighing up of what is best to do. A sinner obviously does what is wrong; however, that person is not simply making the choice to do wrong, but does what is wrong while still in possession of the ethical coordinates in question. Here, then, lies the difference between a violation of the ethical (which amounts to, in good Kantian fashion, a violation of reason itself), and sin: a sinner understands what is wrong, and simply, willfully, does it.

The category of 'sin' now begins to resemble a species of *akrasia*, or weakness of the will. Aristotle was certainly firm in his conviction that akratic behavior cannot be corrected by clearer thinking.[2] Unlike the continent person, who desires to do what is wrong, but does what is right by way of his knowledge of the good, the akratic person really *does* want to do what is best: but he or she[3] simply does something else, and in pain (for example, 'why did I drive through that red light? I knew I shouldn't, and I don't know why I did'). The akratic person's knowledge has not failed: their behavior is itself the (irrational) failure.

There is, however, a far more important observation to be made about how sin is no mere ethical lapse. If we understand human beings

[2] Cf. Donald Davidson's account of weakness of the will (1980: 21–42).

[3] In this case Aristotle can actually accommodate women, since he considered women to be native akratics (e.g. *Politics*, 1260a–25).

simply as ethical creatures, ones obliged to comport themselves in alignment with reason, namely, 'the universal', then that's that: all a person needs to do is to gain some measure of conceptual acuity, reason clearly (or clearly enough) about what to do, and do it. If mistakes are made, a person simply figures out what went wrong, publicly announces his guilt, if necessary, and tries again. The sinner, however, is often utterly invisible to his or her fellow creatures.

How is this possible? In the following way: if a person turns away from their vocation, and fails to commit to their unique life-project, *then that person is also sinning.*

Anti-Climacus wonderfully expresses this thought:

> But ... to be in despair does not mean, although it usually becomes apparent, that a person cannot go on living fairly well, seem to be a man, be occupied with temporal matters, marry, have children, be honored and esteemed—and it may not be detected that in a deeper sense he lacks a self. Such things do not create much of a stir in the world, for a self is the last thing the world cares about and the most dangerous thing of all for a person to show signs of having. The greatest hazard of all, losing the self, can occur very quietly in the world, as if it were nothing at all. No other loss can occur so quietly; any other loss— an arm, a leg, five dollars, a wife, etc.—is sure to be noticed. (SUD, 32)

Despair, claims Anti-Climacus, is sin, and sin is ' ... before God, or with the conception of God, not to will to be oneself ... ' (SUD, 77). Of course, the taxonomy of sin, as explored by Anti-Climacus in *The Sickness Unto Death*, is complicated; I want to focus on this particular dimension of sinning. The striving faithful life is undoubtedly scarred with sin; we now know that one important way for a person to sin is to fall away from her or his uniquely God-given task. How then does that faithful self make repairs? Of course, our tax collector, since he is a self by way of faith, has clearly confessed his sins. This confessional portrait is a very different picture from the happy, absorbed tax collector we have thus far observed.

The Confessional 'Halt'

But before we consider confession, let us acknowledge that we are now about to hear from the Magister himself.

So! At last we meet our elusive host in this house of mirrors, Søren Kierkegaard: he is himself such a religious person, and thinker, and Christian practitioner: so he tells us in *The Point of View* as he concludes his thoughts about his authorship: ' . . . in the world he [Kierkegaard] found what he sought: "that single individual"; if no one else was that he himself was and became that more and more. It was the cause of Christianity he served; from childhood his life was wonderfully fitted for that. Thus he completed the task of reflection—to cast Christianity, becoming a Christian, wholly and fully into reflection. *The purity of his heart was to will only one thing*' (PV, 97, emphasis mine).

That last sentence, of course, is familiar to many who read Kierkegaard's works in English. The first English translation of *Upbuilding Discourses in Various Spirits (Opbyggelige Taler i forskjellig Aand)* was limited to the first section of this lengthy work, and traveled under the misleading title 'Purity of Heart is to Will One Thing'.[4] The correct title of the section in question is 'An Occasional Discourse', and the essay itself is called 'On the Occasion of a Confession: Purity of Heart is to Will One Thing'. The English title, while certainly catchier, is problematic, since it misdirects the reader's attention. 'Purity of heart' is the theme of the occasion (UDVS, 120); it is the occasion, and thus the very reason for the discourse, that should concern us. The occasion is confession.

Let us consider Kierkegaard's account of confession, and see what it can tell us about the faithful existence our tax collector leads.

Kierkegaard makes it clear that confession is not to be undertaken lightly. The precondition for confession is that the repentant person is already an established self. In order to confess truly, the confessor must already have reached a self-reflexive settlement with the opposed dimensions of the human condition. (Two years after the publication of *Upbuilding Discourses in Various Spirits*, Kierkegaard, writing as Anti-Climacus, will famously describe the task of selfhood in *The Sickness unto Death*.[5])

Recall that the latter portion of *An Occasional Discourse* poses a series of questions to such a self. An established self, that 'single individual',

---

[4] See Kierkegaard (1938).

[5] Recall the discussion of how a self is forged in the First Movement.

has realized a God-given birthright: '... at every person's birth there comes into existence an eternal purpose for that person, and that person in particular' (UDVS, 93)—and thus Kierkegaard's query: 'are you now living in such a way that you are aware of being a single individual and thereby aware of your eternal responsibility before God; are you living in such a way that this awareness can acquire the time and stillness and liberty of action to penetrate your life relationships?' (UDVS, 137). That 'single individual', however, must understand that this 'purpose' or vocation is only realized in the tedious and often frayed chores of daily life. Kierkegaard continues to question this 'single individual': is this person wholly committed to that work, despite the difficulties that punctuate every human endeavor: '*In the course of your occupation, what is your frame of mind, how do you perform your work?* Are you convinced that your occupation is your calling so that you do not reinterpret it according to the results and think that it is not still your calling if the results are unfavorable and your efforts do not succeed?' (UDVS, 139). Kierkegaard reminds this person to '... stand fast; by God's help and by your own faithfulness something good will surely come...' The projects of an established self are always conducted in relation to the life-commitment she or he has made, and will continue to make, before God.

The confessor has thus *already* confronted his or her human lot, and taken a stand. The act of confession is not the occasion for realizing or establishing selfhood; rather, only selves have the requisite existential sense that will permit true confession. Near the end of the essay, Kierkegaard remarks: 'But the purpose of the confession is certainly not that a person should become aware of himself as the single individual in the moment of confession and otherwise live without this awareness. On the contrary, in the moment of confession he should as a single individual make an accounting of how he has lived as a single individual' (UDVS, 151). Actual confession can only be undertaken by the 'single individual' to whom the book is dedicated (UDVS, 4).

What then is 'actual confession'? Kierkegaard wants to distinguish the true act of confession from its imitators. Many persons mistake other acts, or conditions, for confession; there are a number of ways, as he puts it, to 'counterfeit eternity' (UDVS, 63), to indulge a mood, a speculative moment, an affect, rather than to confess.

How is a person truly meant to confess? First, actual confession is not contemplation. Kierkegaard uses a map to illustrate the difference:

> Alas, contemplation and the moment of contemplation, despite all its clarity, easily conceal an illusion, because its moment has something in common with the counterfeited eternity... In this it is something like the work of an artist in drawing a map of a country. The drawing of course, cannot be as large as the country; it becomes infinitely smaller, but it also becomes all the easier for the viewer to survey the outlines of that country. And yet if that viewer were suddenly set down in the actuality of that country... he very likely would not be able to recognize the country or gain any notion of it. (UDVS, 72)

Kierkegaard might have spoken more emphatically: especially *because* of its clarity, contemplation seduces the thinker into a sense of having confessed. A contemplative survey of the life-terrain is necessary but, as we should surely suspect, radically insufficient for confession.

Perhaps 'contemplation' fails to produce actual confession because it is too passive, but Kierkegaard also rejects a resolution based on knowledge. Actual confession is not a moment of knowledge-based resolve: 'Perhaps the double-minded person did have a knowledge of the good; in the moment of contemplation it appeared so distinctly before him ... Yes, he felt in his heart as if he must be able to convince the whole world of it' (UDVS, 72). Because the sinner is 'double-minded' (more of this in a moment), the knowledge of the good, as well as the will to do the good, has only the illusion of power. Neither is able to stay the course when the penitent returns to the exigencies of life.

Finally, actual confession is not a burst of desire for the good. 'So perhaps the double-minded person has a feeling for the good, a vivid feeling. If someone speaks about the good, especially in a poetic way, he is quickly moved' (UDVS, 68). But being quickly moved is not enough: 'This is the way feeling tricks the busy person in double-mindedness. After the remorse of a flash of repentance died down in exhaustion, he perhaps had a conviction, so he thought, that there is a mercy that forgives sin; but he himself harshly denied forgiveness to the person who was guilty of something against him' (UDVS, 70). Of course, feeling (remorse, shame, self-loathing) is an important precondition for confession—'Immediate feeling is certainly the first, is the vital force; in it is life ... '; however, Kierkegaard quickly places this feeling in the scheme of things: ' ... but then this feeling must "be kept" ... It must not be left to its own devices' (UDVS, 71). Again, enthusiasm for the good has no staying power when the press of life returns.

The question remains: what is 'actual' confession? The obvious conceptual candidates have been eliminated: a person's quiet review of her or his life from a great height; a private accounting of the facts of one's sin; a sudden passion, a burst of shame at the sight of one's own sinfulness: all of these are, in Kierkegaard's view, a misunderstanding of the act of confession.

Then what is it?

Kierkegaard avers that real confession is a halt.

But what *is* a 'halt', if not contemplation of/knowledge of/desire to be rid of/sin? Are we meant just to *stop* contemplating, desiring, knowing? If so, then the moment looks like a kind of radical syncope, a flash of some manner of not-being. And now the paradox: the 'halt' is *not* a simple cessation. Kierkegaard claims: 'halting is not indolent resting; halting is also movement. It is the heart's inward movement, it is self-deepening in inwardness; but merely to proceed further is the course straight ahead on the surface' (UDVS, 153). The 'course straight ahead' is the path taken by those who misunderstand the nature of confession, those who—in the spirit of Hegel and (more directly) Martensen—argue that the act of confession must have cognitive content, must bring the penitent to a greater understanding of her- or himself.[6] Kierkegaard makes this very clear at the end of the discourse: 'But do not forget that surely the most terrible thing of all is "to go on living deceived, not by what might appear fashioned to deceive, alas, and for that reason dreadfully deceived—deceived by much knowledge. ... " But of what good is it to a person if he goes further and further and it must be said of him, "He is continually going further," when it must also be said of him: There was nothing that halted him?' (UDVS, 153).

---

[6] Bruce H. Kirmmse details Kierkegaard's ongoing conflict with the Hegelians of Copenhagen; he also comments on the particular complaint spelled out in 'An Occasional Discourse' (1990: 280–94). See also Jon Stewart (2003).

The halt is thus not a moment of processing cognitive content; in fact, the halt is inimical to cognition of the usual (or indeed of the lofty) sort. Nonetheless, the halt is absolutely fruitful: 'If you, my listener, know much more about confession than has been said here, as indeed you do, know what follows the confession of sins, this delaying discourse may still not have been in vain, provided it actually has halted you, has halted you by means of something that you know very well, you who know even much more' (UDVS, 153). Notice that knowledge is the *means* to the halt, and not its content, or product. Knowledge of sin must be in place for the halt to happen: the halt is not a further insight into that sinfulness.

Neither is the 'halt' an affect, a suffering sense of one's sin. Kierkegaard makes this clear: 'You are not to withdraw and sit brooding over your eternal accounting, whereby you only take on a new responsibility' (UDVS, 137).

What then is 'the halt'?

First, we should note a kind of homeopathy here. In the prayer that frames[7] the piece, Kierkegaard asks for God's gift of wisdom, sincerity of understanding, and the will to 'will only one thing': the good (UDVS, 7; 154). But the task of willing one thing is 'interrupted' by sin:

> Something came in between; daily, day after day, something intervenes between them: delay, halting, interruption, error, perdition. Then may you give through repentance the bold confidence again to will one thing. Admittedly it is an interruption of the usual task; admittedly it is a halting of work as if it were on a day of rest when the penitent (and only in repentance is the burdened laborer quiet) in the confession of sin is alone before you in self-accusation. (UDVS, 154)

So: the 'halt', the 'interruption' of actual confession, is the only response that can heal the 'halt', the 'interruption' of sin. Feeling remorseful, dwelling on one's transgressions, desiring to will only the

---

[7] The repetition of this prayer is one of the interesting structural features of this piece: the reader, having meditated on 'halting', is evidently better equipped to understand it. Certainly, the very shape of 'An Occasional Discourse' reveals the importance of 'halting': the prose itself quite self-consciously stops in a number of places to review what has already been said (e.g. UDVS, 78; 120; 151).

good: none of these are adequate to repair the rift created by sin—a break must be answered by another kind of break.

What manner of 'break' is the halt?

Our Socratic analogy is once again useful. While the place of arrival for Socrates (knowledge of the good) is of course different from Kierkegaard's goal (repentance of sin), there is a point of contact in their respective undertakings that, I will suggest, illuminates what Kierkegaard is after in actual confession.

As we noted in the First Movement, in the *Meno*, Socrates makes a knowledge claim, that he knows the difference between *orthê doxa*, correct opinion, and *epistêmê*, knowledge (Plato, *Meno*, 98b). So: how do we move from the unreliability of true belief to the security of knowledge? Clearly the true belief must be 'tied down', just as the statues of Daedalus must be tethered lest they run away (*Meno*, 97d–98a). The 'tying down' is a hybrid process; as we see in the slave boy's lesson, it will involve instruction (*pace* Socrates' protestations that he is doing no such thing), practice, and the ability to engage with a true belief from a variety of perspectives: a person must recognize the true beliefs in a multitude of contexts.

But what about the 'moment' when it happens, when the person who holds a true belief comes to know it? Those of us who teach see it all the time. Having explained a concept or an argument for the nth time, a student will suddenly exclaim: 'I get it!' Get what? There is no more content to the concept, or the argument, than there was a moment ago: but something has happened. That elusive, mysterious 'something', the moment of recognition, is that existential collision when a true belief suddenly lands in the right relation to the other (relevant, true) beliefs that the student holds. The student now has knowledge, meaning that she or he can make use of that true belief by way of the whole network of justified true beliefs that constitute that student's knowledge of the world.

I take it that this is part of what Socrates means when he remarks that those who come to have knowledge of virtue do so 'as a gift of the gods' (he surely also ironically means that if Meno were to come to have knowledge of virtue, it would have to be a miracle of this sort). The transition from true belief to knowledge is a mysterious occurrence; it often is an event of the sort just described. A child says that he knows that it is wrong to hit, or to lie, but at some point that child must internalize that belief, see himself as its object, and know that it is so. This event can—and indeed must—be prepared for, but its advent cannot be forced from without.

It is this kind of existential break—a halt, an interruption that has nothing to do with content—that Kierkegaard's actual confession involves.

The comparison here has an appealing symmetry. Socrates' propaedeutic and Kierkegaard's exhortation to confession both map a movement from diremption, from a split, to wholeness. Socrates wishes to mend the division suffered by the putative knower from the correct opinion he precariously holds. Once the interlocutor has recollected, he becomes a whole knower: he is one with the Forms he bears in his immortal soul. Kierkegaard also describes a movement away from a split he calls 'double-mindedness'. He attributes this notion to the Apostle James, and cites the familiar passage: 'Keep near to God, then he will keep near you. Cleanse your hands, you sinners, and purify your hearts, you double-minded' (UDVS, 24). Double-mindedness, however, is *produced by knowledge*:

> In the knowledge, as contemplation and deliberation . . . there presumably is truth, and the knower can understand the truth in it, but he cannot understand himself. It is true that without this knowledge a person's life is more or less devoid of thought, but it is also true that this knowledge, because it is in a counterfeit eternity for the imagination, *develops double-mindedness if it is not honestly gained slowly through purity of the will.* (UDVS, 74, emphasis mine)

Here, despite the symmetry of diremption to wholeness, we leave the Socratic model behind. The condition of double-mindedness is not corrected by the securing of true opinions through recollection; the self made whole is not the knowing self, but the self wholly oriented toward (as opposed to knowing) the good. Healing, however, is only secured by the halt of confession; the healed self has not learned anything, has not 'gone further'. No new knowledge arrives at the moment of confession; no new feelings about sin, or new yearnings to be free of sin, are produced. Certainly, thinking about one's transgressions and the affects and desires that orbit those thoughts are part of the life of a fully realized human self (recall that only selves, those who have negotiated the synthetic nature of being human, are even eligible for actual confession): but such thoughts and feelings are not confession itself.

The nature of confession comes into focus when we compare it to the preparatory work of repentance. Confession is an *event* that is preceded by repentance: repentance is meant to be a 'quiet daily concern' in which the penitent reviews her or his behavior (UDVS, 18). This initial work is necessary for the act of confession to occur: 'Thus repentance must not only have its time, but even its time of preparation . . . it will still be able, well prepared, to collect itself for the solemn occasion also. Confession is such an occasion, the holy act that ought to be preceded by preparation' (UDVS, 19). Repentance—this ongoing reflection on one's transgressions, ebbing and surging with the quotidian tide—finds its fruition in the formal act of confession.

This event, the act of confession, is the moment when doubleness is abolished. Kierkegaard remarks that, in confession, a person achieves 'unity with oneself' (UDVS, 19). This self-union is likened to changing one's clothes:

> Just as a man changes his clothes for a celebration, so a person preparing for the holy act of confession is inwardly changed. It is indeed like changing one's clothes to divest oneself of multiplicity in order to make up one's mind about one thing, to interrupt the pace of busy activity in order to put on the repose of contemplation with oneself. And this unity with oneself is the celebration's simple festive dress that is the condition of admittance. (UDVS, 19)

The image of changing clothes is indeed a strange one: surely a person's clothes suggest doubleness; the naked, actual body is covered, given different dimensions, perhaps even flattered, by an alien garment. Kierkegaard goes on to remark that the quietude of true confession is also like changing one's clothes: 'to take off everything that is noisy since it is empty, in order, hidden in quietness, to become disclosed' (UDVS, 20). The issue is clearly one of harmony, of appropriate dress: the inner intention should be externally worn. Just as a person dons Sunday finery, so too the confessor must wear his or her repentance.[8]

---

[8] Socrates makes a similar remark at the beginning of the *Symposium*: when Aristodemus notices how well dressed Socrates is, Socrates replies that he wants to

What happens during the confession-event that distinguishes it from repentance? We are told that a person 'finds out something' during confession: but this 'finding out' cannot be learning in the ordinary sense; after all, we have already eliminated cognition as a candidate for the defining substance of confession. Kierkegaard claims: 'God does not find out anything by your confessing, but you, the one confessing, do' (UDVS, 23).

In order to get clear about this claim, we should revisit the Platonic analog. When a person recollects, that person now has use of knowledge that, in a sense, *she or he already had*. Of course, in Platonic recollection a shift in cognitive content does occur—a person can now make use of a concept that was previously inaccessible. In confession, however, a person does not have newly retrieved *concepts* at her or his disposal; instead, the facts about one's transgression have been painstakingly gathered by repentance, and are brought to the confessional moment. What the person 'finds out' in confession is something that was already present to her or him in the collection-bag of repentance: but these transgressions are now admitted as part of the very constitution of who one is. I, as a sinner, am not looking on at the rubbish-heap of my failings; I *am* my failings. I am simply a sinner, clothed in my recognition of that sin, standing before God.

The Nietzschean 'Halt'

Confession is the moment of existential ownership. The person confessing is, in that moment, no longer—as Nietzsche famously points out—operating under the seduction of grammar:

> And just as the common people separate the lightning from its flash and take the latter to be a *deed*, something performed by a subject, which is called lightning, popular morality separates strength from the manifestations of strength, as though there were an indifferent substratum . . . but there is no such substratum; there is no being behind the deed . . . the doing is everything.[9]

---

look his best at a party in honor of Agathon (literally, 'the good man') (1989: 3). I will have more to say about the *Symposium* in the Coda.

[9] Nietzsche (1998: 25).

In the collision[10] of confession, a person halts in full ownership of his or her sinfulness. The doubleness of contemplation—I, as a discrete and neutral entity, can survey and consider, feel shameful about, my sin—is gone. In a moment of being hauled up and out of the busyness of the everyday, a person *is* her or his sin. It is a moment of 'recognition', if we hear that word not as a re-cognizing, but as a moment of simply *being* one's sinful self in the presence of God.

Nietzsche also describes a curiously similar existential 'halt'. In *Thus Spake Zarathustra*, a passage from Book IV ('At Noontide') describes this condition:

> About the hour of noon, however, when the sun stood exactly over Zarathustra's head, he passed by an old gnarled and crooked tree which was embraced around by the abundant love of a vine and hidden from itself... Then he felt a desire to relieve a little thirst and to pluck himself a grape; but when he had already extended his arm to do so, he felt an even greater desire to do something else: that is, to lie down at the hour of perfect noon and sleep... In falling asleep, however, Zarathustra spoke thus to his heart: 'Soft! Soft! Has the world not just become perfect? What has happened to me?... Just see—soft! old noontide sleeps, it moves its mouth: has it not just drunk... an ancient brown drop of golden happiness, of golden wine? Something glides across it, its happiness laughs. Thus—does a god laugh... Precisely the least thing, the gentlest, lightest, the rustling of a lizard, a breath, *a moment, a twinkling of the eye*—little makes up the quality of the *best* happiness. Soft! What has happened to me? Listen! Has time flown away? Do I not fall? Have I not fallen—listen! into the well of eternity?[11]

Here we see a moment (*Augenblick*)[12] of transformation in which the world becomes perfect, when Zarathustra momentarily overcomes his

---

[10] Hannay remarks on the importance of the notion of 'collision' in Kierkegaard's writings (2001: 157; 387–9).

[11] Nietzsche (1961: 288).

[12] Cf. 'Øieblikket', the moment described in *Philosophical Fragments* when the disciple and teacher meet: 'And now, the moment... To be sure, it is short and temporal, as the moment is; it is passing, as the moment is, past... and yet it is decisive, and yet it is filled with the eternal. A moment such as this must have a special name. Let us call it: *the fullness of time*' (PF, 18).

disgust at the shortcomings of humanity.[13] This passage contains powerful expressions of completion and affirmation, such as 'perfection' and—more directly for our Kierkegaardian purposes—'eternity'. This is the moment of self-acceptance, the moment when Zarathustra can say 'yes' to himself and in that moment find himself annealed, completed, quenched, finished, his yearning for humanity's distant goal satisfied.

That yearning is for, of course, the Übermensch, that goal towards which human beings are meant to strive. Through the process of constant self-overcoming, by overcoming one's most cherished beliefs, such as the need to affirm a coherent and moral universe, a person will start to make his way across the bridge from 'man' to 'Overman':

> And although you are high and of a higher type, much in you is crooked and malformed. There is no smith in the world who could hammer you straight for me. You are only bridges: may higher men than you step across upon you! You are steps: so do not be angry with him who climbs over you into his height! From your seed there may one day grow for me a genuine son and perfect heir: but that is far ahead. You yourselves are not those to whom my heritage and name belong.[14]

Zarathustra, here in a more characteristic declamatory mood, advocates *not* a sublime instant of self-acceptance, but utter rejection of one's self. Zarathustra denies the way in which both he and these higher men are currently constituted in favor of those who will come later, his 'children'. As he remarks, 'The Overman lies close to my heart, he is my paramount and sole concern—and not man: not the nearest, not the poorest, not the most suffering, not the best'.[15]

---

[13] Kierkegaard makes use of the same noontide trope: 'And the ocean, like the wise man, is self-sufficient . . . or at midday lies, like a half-sleeping indulgent thinker . . . or at night it deeply ponders its own nature . . . the person alone with nature is everywhere surrounded by a totality that does not understand him, even though it continually seems that it might arrive at an understanding . . . infatuated, you drop down beside it; every moment it seems to you as if the explanation has to come in the very next moment, but the brook goes on murmuring, and the traveler at its side only grows older . . . Not so with the one who is confessing' (UDVS, 20–1).

[14] Nietzsche (1961: 293).   [15] Nietzsche (1961: 297).

A free spirit must constantly overcome him or herself. The free spirit struggles to overcome his or her attachments, habits, irrational beliefs, pieces of faith, and so forth, in order to be free of them, and this divestment of self is usually quite painful. In the passage 'Of Self-Overcoming', Zarathustra remarks,

> And life itself told me this secret: 'Behold,' it said, 'I am that *which must overcome itself again and again*.
>
> To be sure, you call it will to procreate or impulse towards a goal, towards the higher . . . but all this is one and one secret . . .
>
> Whatever I create and however much I love it—soon I have to oppose it and my love: thus will my will have it.'[16]

Certainly, the moment of absolute completion is a rare respite for Zarathustra, who is usually caught up in a process of doubleness, of 'constant self-overcoming'. We may well wonder how Zarathustra can possibly reconcile absolute affirmation and self-overcoming: how can the moment in which one wills that everything be eternally the same be *integrated* with a life principled on dissatisfaction? To do or be in one of these dimensions is precisely not to do or be in the other.

This tension is one way of understanding what Zarathustra calls his 'two-fold will': even though he claims that he rejects the all-too-human in favor of the advent of the Übermensch, he also has ties to the realm of self-overcoming, as in 'Of Manly Prudence':

> It is not the height, it is the abyss that is terrible!
> The abyss where the glance plunges downward and the hand grasps upward. There the heart grows giddy through its two-fold will.
> Ah, friends, have you, too, divined my heart's two-fold will? . . .
> My will clings to mankind, I bind myself to mankind with fetters, because I am drawn up to the Overman: for my other will wants to draw me up to the Overman.[17]

Book IV, section 19 offers perhaps the clearest statement of the way in which affirmation is set against overcoming:

> Woe says: 'Fade! Be gone, woe!' But everything that suffers wants to live, that it may grow ripe and merry and passionate, passionate for

---

[16] Nietzsche (1961: 138).   [17] Nietzsche (1961: 164).

> remoter, higher, brighter things. 'I want heirs,' thus speaks everything
> that suffers, 'I want children, I do not want *myself.*'
>
> Joy, however, *does not want heirs or children,* joy wants itself, wants eternity,
> wants recurrence, *wants everything eternally the same.*[18]

Zarathustra's exhortations to overcome ourselves, as well as his more
elusive promises of respite, illumination, and perfection, are inimical:
these notions exclude one another. The great Noontide narcosis, this
epiphany of self-acceptance, is best understood as the moment of
inspiration; as Nietzsche remarks in 'On the Advantages and Disad-
vantages of History for Life':

> ... imagine a man seized by a vehement passion, for a woman or a
> great idea: how different the world has become to him!... It is the
> condition in which one is least capable of being just; narrow-minded,
> ungrateful to the past, blind to dangers, deaf to warnings, one is a little
> vortex of life in a dead sea of darkness and oblivion: and yet this
> condition—unhistorical, anti-historical through and through—is the
> womb not only of the unjust but of every just deed too; and no painter
> will paint his picture, no general achieve his victory, no people attain
> its freedom without... an unhistorical condition.[19]

But this vortex of inspiration must be followed by a struggle to bring
the vision of that moment into reality. The person must return to
history, to the demands and responsibilities of life, to a life of struggle
and self-overcoming.

Clearly, not all halts are created equal. The Zarathustran respite
resembles Kierkegaardian confession, but appearances do deceive.
For Zarathustra, the healing moment is only a refuge from the
double-mindedness of constant self-overcoming: it is not its solution
or resolution. And here we confront a telling, essential difference
between Nietzsche and Kierkegaard: for Nietzsche, doubleness, the
tension of a pair in opposition, is the very pulse of healthy human life.
The dissatisfaction and strife of constant self-overcoming is good and
necessary, as is its narcotic companion, the momentary illusion of
completion. The Nietzsche canon is peopled with doubles who are
fruitful only in the tandem of tension: Apollo and Dionysos, the

---

[18] Nietzsche (1961: 331), additional emphasis mine.
[19] Nietzsche (1983: 64).

Wanderer and his Shadow, the free spirit and the Übermensch. Kierkegaard, however, does promise a kind of completion, one beyond the Zarathustran moment of intoxicated arrival: he does believe that one thing can be willed, and indeed lived.[20] In fact, Kierkegaard diagnoses the Zarathustran individual who caroms between ecstatic self-effacement and the struggles of existence:

> ...the person who effervesces loves the moment, and the person who loves the moment fears time—he fears that the duration of time will make his double-mindedness manifest. And he counterfeits eternity, because otherwise eternity might make it even more manifest. A counterfeiter is he; for him eternity is the bluish boundary of time, for him eternity is the dazzling jugglery of the moment. (UDVS, 62–3)

But not so for Kierkegaard's true confessor. Zarathustra may find *his* eternity in a narcotic break from the demands of life, in the moment's 'dazzling jugglery', but the true confessor will encounter the eternal in everyday life, and in negotiating the demands of the eternal within the temporal. For the true confessor, the doubleness of contemplation is paradoxically resolved in a break, a halt that heals: 'Oh, but it is indeed an interruption that seeks to return to its beginning so that it might rebind what is separated, so that in sorrow it might make up for its failure, so that in its solicitude it might complete what lies ahead' (UDVS, 154). The halt of actual confession provides the penitent with the ability to will one thing, the good. The final lines of Kierkegaard's prayer make clear that the existential halt has the power that human contemplation and desire lack: 'O you who give both the beginning and the completing, may you give victory on the day of distress so that the one distressed in repentance may succeed in doing what the one burning in desire and the one determined in resolution failed to do: to will only one thing' (UDVS, 154).

Communion's Duplexity

Having 'willed one thing' through actual confession, our faithful tax collector is prepared for meaningful prayer, and indeed the taking of

---

[20] Nietzsche also describes a kind of completion and affirmation in his notion of 'constant pregnancy'. For more on Nietzschean 'pregnancy', as well as a complete analysis of Zarathustra's 'Augenblick', see Hough (1997: 85–118).

communion: 'From having made your confession, you go to Holy Communion' (WA, 133). And here we are about to reflect upon a reflection: our tax collector will, oddly enough, look into a mirror, for Kierkegaard's own example of communion is:

Yes! A tax collector, the one described in Luke 18:13, is the focus of Kierkegaard's meditation on the significance of communion.

Here is the verse that becomes the focus of Kierkegaard's analysis: 'And the tax collector stood far off and would not even lift his yes to heaven, but beat his breast and said: "God, be merciful to me, a sinner!"' A comparison of this New Testament tax collector with our own joyful, silent tax collector is surely in order.

Our beloved tax collector of *Fear and Trembling* is, as we have seen, a fascinating study, and his cheerful absorption in the world stands as a challenge to the ways in which we resist and deny our local circumstances. But how does he do it? How can a person come to conduct her or his life in such a way?

The tale of the other tax collector, the one described in *Three Discourses at the Communion on Fridays* (published in 1849), gives us a view inside the *making* of such a person. Johannes de silentio is, perforce, silent on the matter of how his knight forged his faith: he can only observe the creature his imagination has conjured. *Kierkegaard*, however, is absolutely prepared to tell his reader, that 'single individual',[21] about how the tax collector acquired his faith and came 'closest to God': in fact, Kierkegaard remarks that these discourses are 'the resting place of the corpus' (WA, 257).

We now have a frame for thinking about faith's 'knowledge': both tax collectors have faith, and so both are equipped with the kind of 'epistemic flexibility' described in the First Movement. But the tax collector from *Three Discourses at the Communion on Fridays* in the English-edition compilation *Without Authority* ('tax collector WA' hereafter) provides us with a crucial element, one that is missing from our

---

[21] —to whom the 'Confessional Address' of *Upbuilding Discourses in Various Spirits* is dedicated; of this dedication (and those that follow) Kierkegaard remarks, 'the movement is: from the "public" to "the single individual." In other words, there is in a religious sense no public but only individuals' (PV, 10).

cheerful tax collector of *Fear and Trembling* ('tax collector FT').[22] In fact, the mysterious charm of the tax collector FT disguises the radical incompleteness of his story. More needs to be said about sin. God's gifts may be infinitely abundant, but surely sin muddies a person's ability to so see them: where is sin, and its forgiveness, in all of tax collector FT's robust good cheer?

Faith's 'epistemic flexibility'—the knowledge that every gift is good and perfect—is, avers Kierkegaard, made available by communion. The ritual of communion is an event that makes real Christ's sacrifice, and ushers the communicant into the world; the *taking* of communion, however, is a ritual that must be prepared for, one that demands a particular kind of circumspection, or 'sightedness'. The trope of vision does a lot of work in *Three Discourses at the Communion on Fridays*, and it might help to make use of Nietzsche once again: we can foreground the epistemological claims this text is making by way of a comparison with Nietzsche's own epistemological approach. Nietzsche's 'epistemology'—namely, the collection of passages in the corpus that focus on the metaphor of 'perspectivism'—also relies on the trope of eyesight: the nature and limits of our ocular ability become the model for the nature and limits of knowledge.[23] So too for Kierkegaard: the tax collector WA has three moments of vision that inform his faith, that make his faith actual and 'in-the-world'. By attending to what the tax

[22] We might also identify them as 'Rodemester' (so called in *Fear and Trembling*) and 'Tolderen' (from *'Ypperstepræsten'*, *'Tolderen'*, *'Synderinden'*, and *Tre Taler ved Altergangen om Fredagen*, three discourses that are collected along with two other short works in the English edition *Without Authority*). The *Ordbog Over det Danske Sprog* identifies 'Tolderen' as an archaic word for a tariff or customs officer, and lists several instances of it from the New Testament; presumably, Kierkegaard's quotation is taken from his 1820 copy of the New Testament. This twelve-volume set, dubbed the 'blue Testament' because of its blue-green cardboard cover, is currently held by the Royal Library's Kierkegaard Archives; it contains 131 marginal notes by Kierkegaard. Bradley Rau Dewey provides a fascinating account of some of these remarks; he also considers the possibility that 'Kierkegaard could have begun to ponder the theme of "New Testament Christianity" fully five years before he began to write *Training in Christianity*—in fact, the very year he published the aesthetical-ethical volumes called *Either/Or*.'—This reader would add: and indeed in the same year that Kierkegaard published *Fear and Trembling* (1967: 391–409).

[23] Maudmarie Clark gives an excellent account of Nietzsche's perspectivism and his epistemological use of this visual trope (1990: 127–58).

collector WA sees (as well as to that which stands beyond his line of sight), and thus knows, we can finally complete—and understand—de silentio's tantalizing sketch.

The first 'sight' for the tax collector WA is an internal one: 'He would not even lift up his eyes to heaven, but he, who with downcast gaze, turned *in*ward, had only *in*sight into his own wretchedness...' (WA, 130). In seeing his own sinfulness, the tax collector WA is making his confession. As Kierkegaard reminds us in the third of the *Discourses*, 'The Woman Who was A Sinner', confession is terrifying: 'Oh, sin's heavy secret weighs more heavily on a person than anything else; there is only one thing that is heavier—to have to go to confession. Oh, sin's frightful secret is more frightful than any other secret; there is only one thing even more frightful: confession' (WA, 139).

As we have seen, confession is 'frightful' because it is the moment of existential ownership: a person no longer looks on at her or his lapses and failings: a person is *constituted* by those lapses and failings. Confession's 'halt' is the moment when the confessor stops contemplating, or desiring to be rid of, or indeed having knowledge of, his or her sin, and simply *is* a sinful self before God.

Confession thus creates a sanctuary: the confessor stands alone before God: 'At the holy place where everything is quiet, earnest solemnity, and in a more hidden inclosure inside where everything is silence like that of the grave and leniency like judgment on the dead— there the sinner is provided the opportunity to confess his sin' (WA, 139). Here is the second moment of vision, which turns out to be a deepening of the first inward glance: the tax collector WA no longer sees his fellow humans. The confessional space has perspectival boundaries: in order to be (and to see) his sinful self, and to be this self in the presence of God, the tax collector WA cannot see anyone or anything else. 'To make confession is precisely to cast the eyes down, not to want to lift the gaze to heaven, not to want to see anyone else. Indeed, the more honestly you confess, the more you will want to cast your eyes down...' (WA, 133).

The tax collector WA does not see the Pharisee at his side, though the Pharisee certainly sees him, and condemns him: '...the Pharisee saw the tax collector... but the tax collector... did not see the Pharisee. When the Pharisee came home he knew very well that this tax collector had been in church, but this tax collector did not know that the Pharisee had been in church. The Pharisee proudly found satisfaction in seeing the tax collector; the tax collector humbly saw no one . . . with downcast, with inward gaze he was in truth—before God' (WA, 130).

Notice that the sanctuary created by the 'inward gaze' has produced a paradox of distance. Ordinarily, vision establishes a hierarchy of location: the table is near, the window is far, the tree beyond a mere windy blur. So too with how persons locate themselves: here is the choice site (by the beautiful view, or the influential person), and success is a matter of drawing near that which is hierarchically powerful, and thus establishing a place of measurement. The Pharisee, using local human coordinates in order to make his comparison, stands away from the tax collector WA, holds himself higher than him: 'The Pharisee's pride consisted precisely in his proudly using other people to measure his distance from them in his refusing before God to let go of the thought of other people but clinging to this thought in order to stand proudly by himself—in contrast to other people. But that, of course, is not standing by oneself, least of all standing alone by oneself before God' (WA, 129). The tax collector WA, however, is in the sanctuary created by confession: and here the paradox of infinite distance can enter. The distance between the confessor and God is infinite, and immeasurable—nonetheless the confessor is now *closest* to God.

Having made a place in this infinitude, through the work of confession, an astounding final vision is possible: the downcast gaze *sees* God. 'He cast his eyes down, but the downcast gaze sees God, and the downcast gaze is the uplifting of the heart' (WA, 132). The heart's 'uplifting' flows from the act of communion. Of course, the tax collector WA's 'communion' is not the familiar ritual: having abased himself through confession, he can enter the notional space of his own life, the life God intends for him.

The inversion of the tax collector WA's experience—that his self-abasement has the power to bring him into God's presence—is of considerable interest. Sylvia Walsh, in *Living Christianly: Kierkegaard's Dialectic of Christian Existence*, provides a thorough map of Kierkegaard's use of 'inverse dialectic'. Walsh gives the following account of this approach:

> The existential dialectic appropriate to Christianity is informed by a
> peculiar dialectical method and character which Kierkegaard identifies
> as 'inverse dialectic' (*omvendt Dialektik*) or 'the dialectic of inversion'
> (*Omvendthedens Dialektik*). Briefly stated, in inverse dialectic the positive
> is known and expressed through the negative, what appears to be
> negative may be indirectly positive (and vice versa), and the positive
> and the negative, Christianly understood, are always the inverse of the
> natural, human, worldly, and pagan understandings of these terms.[24]

Such an inversion makes possible the tax collector WA's communion:
as Walsh puts it, 'The heightening of the God-relation is achieved by
lowering oneself and becoming as nothing before God'.[25]

Communion, then, is the reassurance that all human suffering—
even the sinful results of negligence and perfidy—can be healed and
made use of in the world: a 'use', we should note, that will ultimately
be discerned by the eternal eye. Walsh remarks:

> The merely human or temporal attitude regards suffering as useful only
> when it can be shown to serve some (temporal) good cause and to be a
> benefit to others. The eternal view sees things *inversely*: the usefulness of
> suffering is determined by whether sufferers are willing to let it help *them*
> to the highest . . . [26]

The final words of the first *Discourse*, 'The High Priest', provide a clear
statement of this transformation: 'Now you go to the Communion
table: the bread is handed to you and then the wine, his holy body and
blood, once again as an eternal pledge that by his suffering and death
he did put himself also in your place, so that you, behind him saved,
the judgment, past, may enter into life, where once again he has
prepared a place for you' (WA, 124).

The communicant has seen God, and—so seeing—is filled with joy:
'Joy and blessing, be assured that you found justification at the
Communion table, that your going there will become a joy and a
blessing to you' (WA, 133).

[24] See Walsh (2005: 7–8).

[25] Walsh (2005: 9). Walsh goes on to adduce the tax collector WA as a
paradigm of 'progress through retrogression'.

[26] Walsh (2005: 117), additional emphasis mine.

Now the tax collector FT's child-like pleasure in his stroll through Copenhagen is no longer simply enigmatic: this affect is profoundly built on the communion before God. The joy of that communion—merely intimated in the behavior of tax collector FT, but borne out in the deeds of tax collector WA—is the wisdom of James 1:17–22: God's love is infinitely abundant, and available at every moment.

Faithful Practices

Faith is characterized by epistemic flexibility and joy: but these are not, as the tax collector FT's behavior might lead us to believe, unintelligible responses of mysterious good cheer. The tax collector FT's investment in the world and the pleasure he takes from it have been hard-earned. The tax collector WA shows us this essential part of the story. He is 'justified' through an exercise in perspective: he must put himself in the right location so that he can successively see, and understand, what is demanded of him.

First, the tax collector WA must put himself 'far off'—the station of confession stands at an utter remove from all human evaluation. Here, alone, he sees his absolute unworthiness.

Contrast this with the Pharisee's location: he knows exactly who he is by virtue of his fellow humans (particularly the tax collector), and he is well-pleased with his social position: 'The Pharisee, however, was not in danger. He stood proud, secure, and self-satisfied; from him no cry was heard. What does this mean? It also has another and totally different meaning: neither was he before God' (WA, 131).

The tax collector WA also knows who he is—absolutely so, for his confession *is* the moment of claiming ownership of every tatty error and ghastly intention, and doing so before God. But the tax collector WA is not pleased with this self—he is horrified, and so he cries out. Kierkegaard describes this moment:

> When you are alone, alone in the place that is more solitary than the desert . . . alone in singleness, or as the single individual, and before God's holiness—then the cry comes by itself. And when you, alone before God's holiness, have learned that it does not help you if your cry were to call any other person for help, that there, where you are the single individual, there is literally no one else but you . . . terror produces this cry, 'God, be merciful to me, a sinner'. (WA, 131)

The tax collector WA has failed to *be himself*. His standing with his family, friends, enemies, colleagues, the entire civic order: all of this is a matter of absolute indifference to him. He has failed himself, and thus failed to bear out the directives of *Styrelsen* (Governance).

This is the place where 'epistemic flexibility' is won. By bringing his sinful self before God in confession, the tax collector WA is now able to see what needs revision (literally), and in turn to see God's infinite capacity to assist in the repair. Of course, this event, the possibility of alteration, is precisely what the Pharisee cannot have. The Pharisee has shut himself off from change: by comparing himself to others, rather than standing before God, he cannot see what needs to be addressed in his life. He is pleased with the finery he has acquired for himself, a judgment made in relation to those around him.

The Socratic analog here is once again irresistible: the tax collector WA arrives at an aporetic juncture; he cannot move forward as he is currently constituted. The very act of confessing that inability is the moment that liberates, just as a Socratic interlocutor must reach *aporia* before he can begin a meaningful search for the answer. Of course, the tax collector WA is not looking for knowledge of his sin—he already has that. What he needs is a way out of his impossible maze of behaviors, and that is what his cry reveals to him: God's infinite transformational power is always already present.

In confession, the location is far off; now, having become whole through confession, the tax collector can draw close in existential communion. Such proximity produces joy—and now the cheerfulness of tax collector FT at last comes into focus. His delight in his immediate, finite circumstances is his thanksgiving, a thanks only made possible by his encounter with God, through confession.

This joy truly is 'against the understanding'; a critical examination of this unconditional embrace of the world can only give us de silentio's baffling sketch. The task, of course, is to *become* that joy. As Kierkegaard reminds us in 'The Lily in the Field and the Bird of the Air':

> What is joy, or what is it to be joyful? It is truly to be present to oneself; but truly to be present to oneself is this *today*, this *to be* today, truly *to be today*. The more true it is that you are today, the more completely present you are to yourself today...Joy is the present time with the

whole emphasis on: *the present time.* Therefore God is blessed, he who eternally says: Today, he who eternally and infinitely is present to himself in being today. (WA, 39)

These words are beautiful and stirring. And now the painful question cannot be put off any longer: what of those for whom being 'present to oneself' is sheer agony? What can we say about human beings who must endure catastrophic privation and abuse? Can these sentiments possibly mean *anything* to someone in this condition?

In what follows, we will struggle with an answer.

6

(In)conclusive Postlude

*On the Absolute Distinction Between Propositional
Beliefs and Walking (or Dancing)*

'Existing is like walking.' *Concluding Unscientific Postscript to the
Philosophical Fragments*, 1:413

Faithful Trembling

The engine that drives the tax collector (as I have already argued in
the First Movement) is Kierkegaard's beloved verse from the Apostle
James: 'Every good and every perfect gift is from above, and comes
down from the Father of Lights, with whom there is no change or
shadow of variation.' The words of James temporally frame *Fear and
Trembling* (as we have already observed, Kierkegaard was composing
three meditations on this verse before and after its composition) and
thus this New Testament passage provides a crucial conceptual back-
drop to this work. I am persuaded that my rapt gaze at our tax
collector, and any subsequent evaluation of his role in *Fear and Trembling*, must place this verse at the heart of that text's complicated,
cantilevered dance.

If so, then we must think more clearly, and carefully, about Kierkegaard's understanding of this verse.

I pause here, if only to confess that in approaching the words of
James I feel very much like a bomb disposal worker: handling this
material can be exceedingly dangerous and perilously misleading.

My apprehension—my fear, and indeed trembling—is well
founded. The words of James are available for (what I will call) cruel
use. How might these words be heard? Here I cannot improve on

Kierkegaard's own analysis, which we considered in the First Movement. But let us review some of the possibilities, all of which are
dismissed by Kierkegaard in the *Upbuilding Discourses*. Consider the
'flatfooted' approach: if 'every gift is good and perfect', then we must
accept whatever comes to us as such. This kind of thought takes a
number of forms; here are three: either 'X is God's will', or 'everything happens for a reason (including X)', or 'something good will
result from X'.

Only those who have lived fortunate, sheltered lives will be able to
stomach these assertions, or their variants. But perhaps not even then:
lives (as yet) unscathed by trauma can imagine what it is like for others,
and feel for them, and make the existential objection that nothing can
(or should be proposed as so doing) assuage, mitigate or explain away
human catastrophe. We see this existential objection in *The Brothers
Karamazov*, when Ivan dialogically tortures his brother, the novitiate
monk Alyosha, into admitting that he would indeed be pleased to see a
general—who had set his hounds on a serf boy, thus tearing him to
bits—shot for his crime.[1] It is worth noting that Dostoyevsky didn't
have to travel far to gather the horrifying tales that Ivan reports to
Alyosha; he gleaned them from the newspapers. Indeed: right now,
the person reading these words can instantly conjure a gallery of
human horrors, either privately experienced or widely known, as a
touchstone for this most human resistance to the lure of explanation.

But let us consider a particular case. In 2010 the novelist Aleksandar Hemon and his wife Teri took their nine-month-old daughter,
Isabel, to the pediatrician for a check-up; the doctor discovered that
her head circumference had deviated significantly from her last measurement. The reason? Isabel was suffering from a rare and devastat-
ingly malignant 'atypical teratoid/rhabdoid tumor', with a survival
rate (for children younger than three) under ten percent. After a long
and agonizing series of treatments, therapies, interventions, and res-
cues, Isabel's tiny body does indeed succumb to her illness (and the
grievous, necessary assaults of her medical rescue effort). Here is what
Hemon has to say to those who would attempt to explain what has
happened to his daughter (and to his family):

---

[1] Dostoyevsky (1950: 288).

One of the most despicable religious fallacies is that suffering is ennobling—that it is a step on the path to some kind of enlightenment or salvation. Isabel's suffering and death did nothing for her, or us, or the world. We learned no lessons worth learning; we acquired no experience that could benefit anyone. And Isabel most certainly did not earn ascension to a better place, as there was no place better for her than at home with her family. Without Isabel, Teri and I were left with oceans of love we could no longer dispense; we found ourselves with an excess of time that we used to devote to her; we had to live in a void that could be filled only by Isabel. Her indelible absence is now an organ in our bodies, whose sole function is a continuous secretion of sorrow.[2]

Hemon's rage at this kind of 'explanatory gambit' is the occasion for our empathy and understanding. It also reminds me—and this is important—of many moments in both the classroom and the scholarly conference session when someone makes a remark of this sort: 'Kierkegaard had better be able to address the issue of suffering in some meaningful way (from e.g. Isabel's terrible death to the Holocaust); otherwise, his work is simply irrelevant.'

An initial answer to these existential demands is simply to return to our analysis of the *Upbuilding Discourses* in the First Movement; here is Kierkegaard's clear statement on the matter: 'And when your allotted portion was sufferings [*Lidelser*] did you thank God? And when your wish was denied, did you thank God? And when you yourself had to deny your wish, did you thank God? And when people wronged and insulted you, did you thank God? *We are not saying that their wrong thereby ceased to be wrong—what would be the use of such pernicious and foolish talk!*' (EUD, 43, emphasis mine)

Kierkegaard is claiming that 'thanking God' (for, of course, 'the good and perfect gift') is *not* thankfulness for suffering, nor for a desire that is unsatisfied (or painfully self-denied), nor is it thankfulness for 'wrongs and insults'. He is quite clear that there is an absolute distinction between a person's rational consideration of her suffering, or injury, and the gratitude that a person gives to God for 'the good and perfect gift'. Putting aside the question of what it *is* that is being received gratefully, we can focus on the difference between what a person suffers and the orientation of thanks.

---

[2] Hemon (2011).

Here, at last, we have an opportunity to return to Abraham. Recall the words of Johannes de silentio: 'Abraham cannot be mediated, which can also be expressed by saying that he cannot speak. As soon as I can speak, I express the universal, and if I do not do that, then no one can understand me' (FT, 52). Silence is necessary, because words are deployed to give reasons, explanations, even comfort (which can be hollow). Language betrays a person's 'subjective inwardness'; as Johannes Climacus puts it,

> Everyone who in truth has ventured his life has had the criterion of silence. A friend can and should never recommend it, quite simply for the reason that the person who, if he is going to venture his life, needs a confidant with whom he will deliberate about it, is not fit for it. But when things begin to be hot, and the final effort is required—then he jumps away, then he seeks relief from a confidant and receives the well-intentioned advice: Be careful of yourself. Then time passes, and the need vanishes. Then when he is visited later by a recollection, he blames people ... But the person who is silent blames no one but himself and affronts no one with his effort, because it is his triumphant conviction that there is and can and shall be in every human being this co-knowledge with the ideal, which requires everything and comforts only in annihilation before God. (CUP, 1:548)

'Silence' thus marks the impossibility of expressing what is essentially a paradox. But this observation is hardly novel: Johannes Climacus, in both the *Philosophical Fragments* and the *Postscript*, reminds us that the God-man is an 'Absolute Paradox', meaning that it cannot be mediated by reason (which does not mean that the notion of the God-man is a logical contradiction, or that this is an irrationalist claim: more of this in a moment).[3] To return to an earlier Johannes, our Johannes of Silence: he too insists that the understanding must not overreach itself in thinking about Abraham. This is the movement from what Johannes de silentio calls 'resignation' to 'faith': a person must achieve 'resignation' before she or he can dwell in faith. As we observed in the 'Breathless Confessional Prelude', a person must become utterly conceptually clear about the contours and limits of her existential situation. A person cannot become faithful without the rational

[3] E.g. C. Stephen Evans's scholarship on this issue (2006: 117–32).

assessment of 'resignation': as Johannes de silentio reminds us: 'Infinite resignation is the last stage before faith, so that whoever has not made this movement does not have faith' (FT, 39). Infinite resignation is necessary precisely because faith is not just another belief, one that (irrationally) trumps the assessment of reason: a person's critical evaluation of what is the case remains the last objective word on the matter. A dead Isaac cannot become 'the seed [from whom] all the nations of the world would be blessed' (FT, 14), and faith is *not* the irrational revolt against this rational conclusion: ' . . . the understanding continued to be right in maintaining that in the world of finitude where it rules it was and remained an impossibility. The knight of faith is clearly conscious of this as well; consequently, the only thing that can save him is the absurd, and this he lays hold of by faith. He therefore acknowledges the impossibility and at the same moment believes the absurd . . . ' (FT, 40). This is what Johannes calls 'the paradox of existence' (FT, 40): at the same moment, reason critically evaluates the scene just as faith urges the person on. The 'absurd', says Johannes, ' . . . does not lie within the proper compass of the understanding. It is not identical with the improbable, the unforeseen, the unexpected' (FT, 39). Within 'the proper compass of the understanding', reason will, and must, deliver a final, objective verdict. Of course, this sentiment is Kantian in its contours; Kant argues that reason has limits, and reason cannot form judgments about matters that lie beyond the phenomenal realm of existence (hence the antinomies that reason falls prey to when it moves beyond its proper domain).[4]

This absolute difference between resignation and faith, held within what Johannes describes as the 'double movement' of faith, anticipates a claim made by Johannes Climacus in the *Concluding Unscientific Postscript*, namely, that there is an absolute distinction between objective truths about reality (propositional claims that can be scrutinized and evaluated), and subjective truth, the relation an individual has to her or his truth claims. To continue with the *Postscript*-language of 'Truth is Subjectivity': objectively, a person living in faith must evaluate and acknowledge the fabric of finitude, the laws of its warp and weft; this is the objective condition, one always available to reason.

---

[4] Kant (1965: 422–35).

Subjectively, a person 'believes' in the conceptually thin/existentially rich notion that 'every gift is good and perfect'. This 'belief' is characterized not as a thought, but as an action: in his meditation on the James verse, Kierkegaard argues that the 'wrong' suffered must be 'taken to God': '. . . have you *taken* the wrong and insult to God and by your thanksgiving received it from his hand as a good and perfect gift?' (EUD, 43, emphasis mine). Notice that the faithful sufferer does not reevaluate her condition, but 'takes' it to God for transformation. Objectively, the faithful sufferer remains in a grievous condition; subjectively, the faithful sufferer has, through 'thanksgiving', received God's blessings.

These two 'conditions' have their respective, native tools of evaluation, and they exist in a tension. Objectively, a person must draw rational conclusions about her environment, her culture, about the laws of nature, and the evidence of the historical record; subjectively, the faithful person must move forward.

Literally. Consider Abraham: he does not waste time in imagining a resurrected Isaac, or even a reprieved one: in the Genesis account, Abraham rises early, saddles his donkey, splits wood for the burnt offering, and begins his journey to Mount Moriah. The scene is silent. Abraham—apart from the refrain of 'Here I am'—does not speak,[5] nor are we privy to any of his thoughts. Abraham moves through the world, each moment of his journey a faithful dwelling in the 'goodness of what is', rather than a speculative evaluation of what must come.[6] Of these verses Johannes de silentio remarks, '. . . the journey lasted three days and a good part of the fourth; indeed, these three and a half days must be infinitely longer than the couple of thousand years that separate me from Abraham' (FT, 45). Did Abraham find these days torturously long? He does not say, and his regular gait indicates nothing. But surely he knows what must come, and what he will catastrophically do?

Yes. Abraham's task—the sacrifice of Isaac—is the objective condition of his journey. What God demands, Abraham will provide, and

---

[5] —Apart from his reply to Isaac: more about this utterance in what follows.

[6] Genesis 22:1–4.

Abraham knows full well what that sacrifice entails. He is resigned to what he must do, and he knows that he will do it.

The subjective condition of Abraham's assignment is, however, the double movement of faith. Notice that Abraham does not bargain, plead, lament his fortune or even offer himself as sacrifice; all of those responses belong to the objective condition, which is already a matter settled by reason. Abraham simply begins to move towards that fatal reckoning, *which is not entertained as a fatal reckoning* as he gathers the wood or prepares his donkey: then again, Abraham's absorption in what he does suggests that he 'entertains' very little. Abraham is faithfully present in each moment of work, and that work is move-ment, each bodily effort an expression of faith.

Faithful Belief

I have described the orientation of the subjective condition as a 'belief', but in fact even a conceptually thin 'belief' such as the James verse may be too 'objective' for the activity of faith. Johannes de silentio describes the condition of the resigned believer: ' . . . even if madness held up a fool's costume before my eyes and I understood by its look that it was I who should put it on, I can still save my soul if I am otherwise more anxious that my love for God rather than my worldly happiness triumphs in me. Even at the last moment a person can concentrate his whole soul into one single glance *toward that heaven from which all good gifts come* . . . then he will calmly put on the costume . . . But by my own strength I cannot get the least bit of what belongs to finitude, for I continually use my strength to resign everything' (FT, 42, emphasis mine). Notice the embedded paraphrase of the James verse; clearly, here the *thought* of God's 'good and perfect gifts' becomes one of resignation. The belief that governs the movement of faith can be *articulated* as the James verse, but it is *expressed* by a way of moving through the world. 'Temporality, finitude is what it is all about': how Abraham spends his time as he makes his way to Mount Moriah (absorbed in his task at each moment) and his constant orientation toward the infinitely abundant goodness of the finite world around him (he ' . . . does not lose the finite but gains it entire') are the substance of his faith. In this sense, faith is a *doing*, and not a thought about what one does. It is obvious that a belief (one that clearly anticipates the James verse) is what guides and informs the doing: but the belief as rendered objectively misdescribes its subjective reality. Johannes de silentio draws this conclusion about the belief that animates Abraham: 'Abraham believed. He did not believe that he would be blessed one day in the hereafter but that he would become blissfully happy here in the world. God could give him a new Isaac, call the sacrificed one back to life. He believed by virtue of the absurd, for all human calculation had long ago ceased' (FT, 30). Objectively, there is nothing left to calculate; subjectively, Abraham must move through the world dwelling in the infinite goodness available to him from moment to moment.

This characterization of faith's 'double movement' as objective rational assessment and attendant resignation, which at the same time subjectively embraces and indeed (literally) embodies infinite possibility ('With God all things are possible'), is not as strange a phenomenon as it might sound. In fact, it is often heard from those who have endured terrible trauma and loss: objectively, it was impossible to survive, but 'somehow' that person manages to keep going—'I kept putting one foot in front of the other' is the conventional remark. Of course, such reports can sound like numb endurance; faith, however, is inherently joyful. Recall Johannes de silentio's description of Abraham when Isaac is spared: '[he is] delighted to receive Isaac back, truly inwardly delighted, and [needed] no preparation, no time to collect himself in *finitude and its joy*' (FT, 30, emphasis mine). Indeed, 'the joy of finitude' is already available to Abraham, through faith.

So what is it that Abraham believes? The path he faithfully walks to Mount Moriah is, says Johannes, traversed 'by virtue of the absurd' (FT, 29); it is not, however, the case that Abraham believes something that is nonsensical or a contradiction. He does believe, and accept, that the sacrifice is commanded; he also believes God's promise that Isaac is the gift that will bless 'all the generations of the world' (FT, 14). This is Abraham's objective condition. Subjectively, he is bound up in his task, from moment to moment, neither anticipating nor regretting. Abraham refrains from speculation and grievous affect, and simply moves forward into his task. C. Stephen Evans remarks, 'I conclude that Abraham does not, at the crucial time, hold the contradictory belief that he will and will not sacrifice Isaac ... Abraham simply rests unwaveringly in his trust in God's goodness; he believes that God will keep his promise to him in this life, even though he does not know exactly how God will do this, and realizes that from the perspective of human experience it looks impossible' (FT, xix). I would alter Evans's commentary only slightly: Abraham does not *rest* in God's goodness; rather, he *walks* in absorbed concern, a kind of existential focus made possible by God's goodness as orientation and guide. As Johannes Climacus observes in the *Postscript*: 'But truly to exist, *to permeate one's existence with consciousness*, simultaneously to be eternal, far beyond it, as it were, and nevertheless present in it and nevertheless in a process of becoming—that is truly difficult... To think existence *sub specie aeterni* and in abstraction is essentially to annul it... Existence without motion is unthinkable, and motion is unthinkable *sub specie aeterni*... Existence, like motion, is a very difficult matter to handle' (CUP, 1: 308, emphasis mine). Here an obvious phenomenological observation is available to us: to 'permeate one's existence with consciousness' is surely not to live by means of an explicitly entertained set of beliefs, but to embody, and carry out, a vocation in the world that is constantly refreshed by habits and skills that are attuned to the availability of the world, namely, 'God's goodness'.

Heliotropic Silence

Abraham, as he makes his way to Mount Moriah, believes that he must sacrifice Isaac according to God's command; he also trusts that God will (somehow) not take Isaac from him, according to his promise. His comportment belies this terrible situation: Abraham moves towards the fateful encounter in rapt silence. When he does speak, as Johannes de silentio notes, 'he does not say anything... His reply to Isaac has the form of irony, for it is always irony when I say something and yet do not say anything.' Abraham tells Isaac that 'God himself will provide the lamb for the burnt offering, my son!' (FT, 104–5). What, therefore, has Abraham actually said? Johannes identifies this moment as evidence for the 'double movement' of faith: Abraham knows that he must sacrifice Isaac—first movement—but he then moves forward with the certainty that he will keep Isaac— second movement. Abraham carries Isaac in that tension between his objective condition and his subjective dwelling in 'every good and perfect gift'.

The words of the Apostle James are proleptically present (that is, as Johannes tells the tale) in the Abraham story. James warns his readers to be 'quick to hear' and 'slow to speak': surely Abraham's silence—and indeed the silence at work in what he *does* say—anticipates this New Testament verse. But his silence is also that of the rapt practitioner in a sunlit sanctuary. Remember that the James verse begins as follows: 'Every good and perfect gift is from above, and comes down from the Father of Lights, with whom there is no change or shadow of variation.' In one of his 1843 meditations on this verse, Kierkegaard remarks, ' "From the Father of lights," says the apostle, and thereby signifies that God penetrates everything with his eternal clarity . . . ' (EUD, 39). Abraham's subjective condition is to dwell in the full radiance of God's love, the eternal, comprehensive and unvarying light of unshadowed noon; Abraham moves forward in the presence of this kind of light, one very different from reason's clinical lamp, able only to reveal what is, and is not, the case. Abraham's path is illuminated in a way that the gaze governed by beliefs and desires, and its attendant critical evaluation, cannot see. Rational appraisal sees opportunities and potential rewards, or perhaps disappointment and, on a regular basis, disaster. For the faithful person, that calculation of what is the case, and what can never be, takes place in an arena limned with the assurance of 'good gifts' and promise of abundant life.

Obviously, these remarks do not answer the question with which we began: how does the phenomenon of faith address the manifold misery, disaster, and horror of human life?

Of course, the question—asked in this way—is itself the problem. In fact, we are missing a crucial part of Kierkegaard's account, one that will bring the life of faith into sharper focus.

The Faithful Sufferer

Faith is, above all, realized in the encounter of a self with its Source (SUD, 14), and a self is forged in the consciousness of existing before God: 'the greater the conception of God, the more self there is; the more self, the greater the conception of God' (SUD, 80). A self has a vocation, her unique work in the world, and faith is the activity of making that work manifest.

Consider our tax collector, who clearly inhabits the world in a way that is very different from most human beings: that 'way' is faith, and faith is the lived activity of the self. This self is forged in a commitment to a vocation (we know not what; remember that he only *looks* like a tax collector); that absolute commitment ('infinite passion', in de silentio's terms) creates a host of existential capacities: the tax collector dwells in the moment, finds infinite joy in his finite circumstances; the world through which he moves is made manifest as comprehensively abundant. These abilities, as we saw in the Fourth Movement, are made possible by the lived practices of the confessional 'halt', by 'existential' communion (so called because the tax collector in Luke 18:13 is an anticipatory exemplar of lived communion), and through prayer.

These practices become the engine that drives the faithful life, and they can certainly be understood as analogous to the practices of, say, a Buddhist or Christian contemplative who has become an adept: through guided meditation, or inner recollection, that person is released from the tendency to grasp at his material condition, and hence from an attachment to things, and, of course, from the suffering that 'grasping attachment' brings.

Here the comparison with Buddhism is of some interest: of course, the absolute desideratum of Buddhism (and, indeed, the point of the Four Noble Truths and the Eightfold Path) is the cessation of suffering. Kierkegaard has much to say about Christian suffering, and it will be useful to compare his remarks with those of this utterly different religious tradition.

The goal of Buddhism is to achieve 'the total calming of suffering'.[7] Of course, 'suffering', *duḥkha*, is a multivalent term, one that includes all manner of worry, anticipatory discomfort, and actual physical pain. Grief about what one has lost can be painful; so too is gaining what one does not expect or want, or indeed the expectation of such loss or gain. Most importantly, there is an ontological discomfort present in all sentient beings: existence itself cannot deliver on the promises of pleasure or the demands of desire. The path of

---

[7] See Morris (1989–1995: II.52). Thanks to Christian Coseru for his insightful comments in our discussions about Buddhism and suffering (see Coseru (2012)).

contemplative cultivation can provide a newly awakened conscious-ness with the mindful tools to transcend suffering, or perhaps to transform it.

The conjunction here could not be more startling. The Buddhist begins with the assertion that human suffering is the condition that is to be eliminated; Kierkegaard, in his final set of polemical pamphlets, *The Moment*, has much to say about the *importance* of suffering in the life of the faithful Christian.

We should stop to consider these pamphlets, written at the very end of Kierkegaard's life, and their target: the Danish Lutheran Church. From December 1854 to the posthumous issue[8] of *The Moment* no. 10, the accusations grow increasingly shrill: the non-existence of New Testament Christianity (TM, xxix, 39) is the fait accompli of 1800 years of hypocrisy (TM, 134–5, 226), culminating in the 'criminal case' (TM, 129, 166) of the Church's pastors, sporting the long robes of professional Christians—'there is something dubious about men in women's apparel', Kierkegaard remarks—all the while dispensing sugary homilies, presiding over theatrical rituals (TM, 221, 230, 249) like waiters (TM, 106) serving palliatives; Kierkegaard likens their behavior to perjury (TM, 253), counterfeiting and fraud (TM, 129), murder (TM, 150), and cannibalism (TM, 321); 'Every Sunday divine worship [makes] Christianity . . . a game and a fool is made of God' (TM, 168).

And what is the fundamental error here? The clergy has obscured the actual message of New Testament Christianity, that Christians are called to 'hatred of self' (TM, 4, 17, 47, 168, 184, 189) and 'suffering': 'God is speaking about suffering and hunger, thirst and cold and nakedness and imprisonment and flogging' (TM, 22); to be a Chris-tian, he concludes, 'is sheer agony' (TM, 189). God can only be loved in suffering (TM, 294) and, in making these demands, God becomes 'your mortal enemy' (TM, 178). Christianity as it is practiced in Denmark, Kierkegaard concludes, is about 'the enjoyment of life' (TM, 42), and 'securing conveniences, profit, earthly goods' (TM, 32); 'Christendom' is as disanalogous to Christianity as enjoyment is to suffering (TM, 52).

---

[8] This issue of *The Moment* was not published until 1881.

And what was the official response from the Danish Lutheran Church to Kierkegaard's attack? Bishop Martensen's reply to Kierkegaard's initial salvo in the *Faedrelandet* is both self-righteous and careful (as if to signal the degree to which Kierkegaard has become unhinged[9]): Martensen argues that Kierkegaard misunderstands the truths of the Christian church, which are not only for 'extraordinary times'; Martensen argues that he lacks 'congregational consciousness' (TM, 362): 'Kierkegaard's faith ... is not at all the faith of a community but solely and simply a private religion' (TM, 364). As for the imperative of suffering, Martensen concludes: '... it must be herewith pointed out that many zealots and fanatics have also undergone great sufferings without therefore being truth-witnesses. Furthermore, what justifies his overlooking the fact that there are sufferings other than tangible persecution? ... Dr. S. Kierkegaard must ... be so obsessed by a *fixed* idea that he has eventually lost the simplest presence of mind ...' (TM, 362).

Martensen's objection to the imperative of suffering is worth considering. After all, suffering *simpliciter* is obviously not the point of Kierkegaard's depiction of Christianity: he reminds his reader to '... take care that time does not go by unused, perhaps in *useless* suffering ...' (TM, 295, emphasis mine). Mere insult, illness, accident or assault—indeed all the rich variety of human pain, from the material (disability, poverty) to the affective (envy, thwarted ambition, jilted love), are *in themselves* irrelevant to the task of becoming a Christian; instead, he instructs us (in proleptically Nietzschean terms) to resolve to 'will to suffer' (TM, 294).

What is the 'will to suffer', and how does it lead us to the right kind of 'hatred of self', one that informs a truly Christian life? What will that life look like?

As we saw in the Second Movement, *Either/Or I* is the pastiche-tale of the aesthete A's manifold, desperate gambits to secure pleasure— 'enjoyment', as Judge William puts it—and how that pursuit paradoxically turns into *suffering*. A has taken a remarkable journey: in

---

[9] Kierkegaard himself admits that his invective is surely heard as a kind of lunacy (TM, 206, 320, 334, 340).

his efforts to commit to pleasure (from the 'Diapsalmata' to 'the Unhappiest One', to the involutions of Johannes the Seducer's diary), he ends up finding his substance and meaning in unhappiness.

A's embrace of suffering is, of course, *not* 'the will to suffer'; in fact, it is an example of the 'useless' suffering Kierkegaard warns his readers about. How, then, to suffer in the right way? How does a person 'suffer Christianly'?

One hint here is another element of Kierkegaard's entreaty: a person must develop a 'hatred of self'. Self-hatred, of course, *necessarily presupposes a self*; only established selves are able to suffer in the right way.[10] This self, as we have seen, is not a static creation; rather, it is a dynamic, existential expression, at every moment dying to immediacy in order, paradoxically, to live the life intended for that 'single individual':

> One lives only once. If when death comes your life has been used well—that is, used so it rightly relates itself to eternity—God be eternally praised . . . he would like you finally to will what he for the sake of eternity wills for you: that you might resolve to will to suffer, that is, that you might resolve to will to love him, because you can love him only in suffering, or if you love him as he wills to be loved you will come to suffer. (TM, 294)

George Pattison, in *Kierkegaard's Upbuilding Discourses*, provides this discerning explanation of religious suffering: 'Suffering . . . is more a kind of self-consciousness, a feeling about how one's life in the world is constituted, a form of inwardness. So, for the religious individual, suffering is simply *a way of being in the world*.'[11] In what follows, I will build on Pattison's phenomenological characterization of 'Christianly suffering'.

---

[10] Here again it is tempting to draw the comparison with canonical Buddhist practice: the transformation and subsequent release of the Buddhist practitioner hinges on a recognition of 'no-self': there is no subject or agent who possesses these states. Kierkegaard's notion of 'hatred of self' might be fruitfully compared to the Buddhist's insistence that a person let go of all conventional notions of her personhood, ones that foster an unhealthy attachment to the passing scene.

[11] Pattison (2002: 27), emphasis mine.

Christian Selves

This understanding of selfhood—that a self is forged insofar as it is able to die to itself, that a person finds his or her unique vocation in the world by renouncing and turning away from worldliness—is of course an example of the inverse dialectic that characterizes Kierkegaard's account of Christianity. Recall our discussion of 'inverse dialectic'[12] in the Fourth Movement, and its clear promise: *actual* joy and comfort are available, but only through the self's death to its own immediacy. This 'death' or self-denial is absolutely specific: only the 'single, solitary' petitioner engaged in ongoing self-confrontation can become aware of the unique demands of her or his own existence. The suffering that a person endures in the name of truth, that is, the truth of his or her own subjectivity, is what makes possible *Christian* joy and comfort: 'But first and foremost, are you on good terms with God, are you considering this quite earnestly, are you honestly trying to understand—and this is God's eternal changeless will for you as for every human being, that one should strive for this—are you honestly striving to understand what God's will *for you* should be?' (TM, 272, emphasis mine).

It is this objective, Kierkegaard insists, that the clergy has covered up: by focusing on thanksgiving, redemption, and the promised comfort of God's love, the congregants are distracted from the real issue, namely, the way in which *actual* comfort (and redemption, and likewise authentic praise) is achieved: through selfhood. Certainly, as long as 'congregants' see themselves *as such*—identifying themselves primarily as members of a group—they will be unable to become aware of themselves in this crucial way, as potential *selves*: 'This is the purpose of the whole machinery of a state Church and 1000 royal officeholders, who in the guise of the care of people's souls cheat them out of

---

[12] Sylvia Walsh remarks: 'There are essentially four basic and decisive negative qualifications of Christian existence that must be viewed and correlated in the dialectical manner just described. These are the consciousness of sin, the possibility of offense, dying to the world or self-denial, and suffering. Through these negative qualifications Christian strivers stand related to or bring to expression in their existence the positive qualifications of Christianity: faith, forgiveness, new life, love, hope, joy and consolation' (2005: 14).

the highest in life—the coming into existence of *self-concern* within them . . . ' (TM, 159, emphasis mine).

Authentic self-concern is occluded by the false notion of 'self' that is promoted and administered by the state Church, a 'self' understood numerically and homogeneously, one like the others, one among others. This inauthentic understanding of self allows the congregant to avoid confronting his or her own existential need for actual self-hood: ' . . . now, instead, the need (and the coming into existence of this very need is life's highest meaning) does not come into existence at all, but by being satisfied long before it has come into existence is hindered in coming into existence' (TM, 159).

Kierkegaard calls his readers to become aware of their existential condition: 'Was I not right, and am I not right, that first and foremost everything must be done to have it definitely determined what is required in the New Testament for being a Christian, that first and foremost everything must be done so that we are at least able *to become aware*?' (TM, 29, emphasis mine).

Kierkegaard's full-throated paean to suffering is, therefore, only half of the story. By the lights of his inverse dialectic, we may only achieve the joy of being Christian by means of self-abnegation and suffering. Yet the question remains: why then is there so little said in these final pamphlets about the joyful life this suffering provides? The depiction of Christian life in *The Moment* is unrelievedly grim; even the conventionally worthy tasks of marriage and child-rearing are held in contempt: 'I honestly do not comprehend how it has occurred to anyone to want to link being a Christian with being married . . . *Christianly* it is anything but the greatest good deed to give a child life . . . '; in fact, 'Christianly there is no family life' (TM, 239, 250, 252). Instead, Kierkegaard avers that 'what God wants—out of love—is that a person shall die to the world, that if God is so gracious as to turn his love toward him, that what God then does—out of love—is to torment him in all the agonies designed to take life away from him, because it is this that God wants . . . he wants to have the life of the one who is born, wants him transformed into one who has died, someone who lives as one who is dead . . . ' (TM, 251).

In evaluating the extremity of such remarks, Walsh observes: 'Numerous interpreters have found Kierkegaard's attitude in his last writings to be radically negative and world-denying . . . however, such a culmination would represent not the logical conclusion of his central vision but rather an abrogation of it...His foremost intent was to assert the positive in and through the negative, not to advance a purely negative characterization of Christian existence.'[13]

A 'world-affirming' characterization of the Christian life is precisely what Kierkegaard denies in *The Moment*; however, he does insist that 'the will to suffer' produces an authentically Christian joy. We can sharpen our understanding of this suffering and its joy by paying attention to a specific textual cue, one that plays an important role in both the first and secondary authorship of Kierkegaard.

Dancers and Bureau(crat)s

Kierkegaard's message is clear: we must suffer in the right way to become Christian. The 'right' kind of suffering is, of course, the suffering of the faithful self. Kierkegaard evidently intends his vitriol to cauterize, not to burn: he presents his readers with a 'radical cure' (TM, 17). This approach does not advocate suffering *simpliciter*, nor does it misunderstand the attractions of an easier life:

> Far be it from me to speak disparagingly of comfort! But let it be used, wherever it can be used, only in relation to everything that is something in such a way that this something is indifferent to the way in which it is had, so that one can have it both in one way and in another, because when this is the case, the convenient and comfortable way is undeniably preferable. For example, water. Water is something that can be obtained in the hard way by fetching it from the pump, but it also can be obtained in the convenient way by high pressure; naturally I prefer the convenient way. But the eternal is not something like that, indifferent to the way in which it is obtained; no, the eternal really is not a something but is—*the way in which it is obtained*. The eternal is obtained in only one way—and it is precisely in this that the eternal is different from everything else, that it can be obtained in only one way. (TM, 110, emphasis mine)

The 'eternal' is obtained by achieving selfhood, but the established self does not exist in a static state; rather, that self is maintained through

---

[13] Walsh (2005: 160).

faithful engagement with the world: the 'way' that the eternal is obtained *just is* this activity.

But what does that sustained, faithful life *look* like?

Kierkegaard offers a telling comparison: 'What we call a teacher in Christianity (pastor) no more resembles what the New Testament understands by a teacher of Christianity than a chest of drawers resembles a dancer' (TM, 53).

This trope is instructive. First, consider the phenomenological implications of being 'bureau-like'—after all, what are bureaus for? Storage, of course: and so the pastor-as-storage, the bureau(crat), is merely a repository of useful homilies and ritual blessings, neatly folded and ready to be used. A chest of drawers is meant to keep its contents organized and well out of sight (no need to have stacks of socks and underclothing out in the room). The pastor-bureau(crat) is thus essentially a managerial device: here are comforting, helpful formulae (the christening, the sermon, the wedding ceremony, the funeral) that are available as needed, and put away when not. There is thus a distinction between the bureau(crat) and the material he stores; what is dispensed on Sunday is put away on Monday. This lacuna, the bureau(crat)'s distance from the pastoral wisdom he dispenses, is precisely what most infuriated Kierkegaard about Bishop Mynster:

> ... in the hands of Governance I became the occasion for Bishop Mynster to pronounce judgment upon himself: his sermon on Sunday he either did not recognize or dared not or would not acknowledge on Monday... If on Monday Bishop Mynster had not himself worldly-sagaciously avoided taking the consequences of his Sunday sermon, if he had ventured an existence and actions that corresponded to the rhetoric of the Sunday discourse instead of availing himself of different models—his life would also have come to look entirely different. (TM, 13)

Kierkegaard wanted Mynster—as he now urges his readers—to *live* the words of the New Testament, rather than merely dispensing them: to be dancers, not storage units. Yeats' famous lines from 'Among School Children' deftly spell out Kierkegaard's meaning: 'O body swayed to music, O brightening glance/How can we know the dancer from the dance?'[14] The dance is nothing more than its expression in

---

[14] Yeats (1996: 215).

the moment: the choreography guiding the dancer is merely the plan, not in any sense actual *dancing*.

Consider also what it is like to be a dancer engaged in a dance. The dancer must be utterly committed to and focused on the body's movements; this person does not do something in addition to or besides the dance, if he or she is really to *dance* (it cannot be 'both-and' (TM, 101, 425); the dancer is completely absorbed in the dance as it happens. The floor may be uneven in spots, the room may become too hot or too cold, the foot may catch and the body stumble: a dancer cannot and does not anticipate what may come. Adjustments are made as the dance is danced out, not plotted out beforehand.

These qualities—the existential nature of dance itself, the dancer's absorption and temporal focus (the 'Here I am' of Abraham's refrain (FT, 21))—are familiar to us from the opening meditation of *Fear and Trembling*. Recall Johannes de silentio's description of the difference between the knight of resignation and the knight of faith: 'The knights of infinity are ballet dancers and have elevation ... But every time they come down, they are unable to assume the posture immediately, they waver for a moment, and this wavering shows that *they are aliens in the world* ... But to be able to come down in such a way that instantaneously one seems to stand and to walk, to change the leap into life into walking, *absolutely to express the sublime in the pedestrian*—only that knight [of faith] can do it, and this is the one and only marvel' (FT, 40–1, emphasis mine).

Here we have two dancers, both expert in the movements of infinity: both the knight of resignation and the knight of faith know 'the blessedness of infinity', and both of them have 'felt the pain of renouncing everything' (FT, 40)—but the knight of faith has a different skill, that of embodied, finite, temporal expression: this knight ' ... grasped everything again by virtue of the absurd. He is continually making the movement of infinity, but he does it with such precision and assurance that he continually gets finitude out of it ... ' (FT, 41).

The resigned Christian and the faithful Christian are thus distinguished by their ability to live out their infinite passion in this world. Kierkegaard, writing in *The Moment*, seems to be speaking with the voice of resignation when he argues that 'a Christian in the New Testament sense is completely alienated from this life. He is, as it says in Scripture... a stranger and an alien... he feels himself a stranger, and everyone feels instinctively that he is a stranger to him' (TM, 257). This verse (I Peter 2:11) is also quoted by Johannes de silentio: 'the knight of faith is the only happy man, the heir to the finite, while the knight of resignation is a *stranger and an alien*' (FT, 50, emphasis mine).

The knight of infinite resignation's awkward inability to 'express the sublime in the pedestrian' is strikingly present in Kierkegaard's final writings. Kierkegaard understands the enormity of the sacrifice demanded by New Testament Christianity, and he tirelessly exhorts us to despise ordinary life and its preoccupations: 'What Christianity requires for saving one's life eternally... hating one's own life in this world—is there a single one of us whose life even in the remotest manner can be called even the weakest striving in this direction...?' (TM, 47). As we have already observed, this 'hatred of one's own life' includes marriage ('In God's Word celibacy is recommended') and having children: 'Christianly, it is anything but pleasing to God that one engages in begetting children... Christianly, it is the highest degree of egotism that because a man and a woman cannot control their lust another being must therefore be born into this vale of tears ...' (TM, 250–1). Kierkegaard calls his readers to give up the world, not to marry, not to have children: but this, according to Johannes de silentio, is the voice of infinite resignation:

> The act of resigning does not require faith, for what I gain in resigna-tion is my eternal consciousness, and this is a purely philosophical movement which I... can discipline myself to do. For whenever some-thing finite gets beyond my control, I starve myself until I make the movement, for my eternal consciousness is my love for God, and for me that is higher than anything... By resignation I renounce everything... (FT, 41)

The knight of faith, on the other hand—indeed, our tax collector!—'gets the girl':

> By faith I do not renounce anything; on the contrary, by faith I receive everything, exactly in the sense in which it is said that one who has faith like a mustard seed can move mountains... it takes a paradoxical and humble courage to grasp the whole temporal realm by virtue of the absurd, and this is the courage of faith... By my own strength I can

give up the princess, and I shall not become a sulker but find joy and peace and rest in my pain ... But by faith, says that miraculous knight, by faith you will get her by virtue of the absurd. Alas, this movement I cannot make ... And yet it must be glorious to get the princess. (FT, 41–2)

Kierkegaard, as he presents himself in *The Moment,* cannot 'grasp the whole temporal realm' as Johannes de silentio here describes it: he cannot do so because the Kierkegaard of the second authorship is appropriating the temporal from the vantage point of eternity. At this point the resources made available by de silentio's account grow thin, since his focus is avowedly finite and temporal; let us once again celebrate de silentio's succinct observation: 'Temporality, finitude— that is what it is all about' (FT, 42). Thus Kierkegaard, writing in *The Moment,* can still admire a love that is all-encompassing, but he now judges this love in the light of one's eternal relationship with God: 'The Christianity of the New Testament would be: if that man actually could love in such a way that with the passion of his whole soul the girl truly was the one and only beloved ... then, hating himself and the beloved, to let the girl go in order to love God' (TM, 184). This shift in perspective is made clear in an earlier remark from 'The Gospel of Sufferings':

> When the well-to-do person is riding comfortably in his carriage on a dark but starlit night and has the lanterns lit—well, then he feels safe and fears no difficulty ... But just because he has the lanterns lit and has a strong light close by, he cannot see the stars at all. His lanterns darken the stars, which the poor peasant, who drives without lanterns, can see gloriously in the dark but starlit night. (UDVS, 310)

The immediate absorption that characterizes the temporal interferes with the view of eternity:

> With all kinds of clever inventions of comfortability, they want to teach people to make it as bright as possible around them in temporality so that they would no longer be able to see eternity. Or even if they do not want to do away completely with the conception of eternity and the happiness of eternity, they still want to degrade it in such a way that no eternal difference (indeed, what could be more meaningless) remains between the temporal and the eternal ... there must be an eternal difference between the temporal and the eternal. (UDVS, 310)

This is why, in *The Moment*, Kierkegaard reminds his reader that '... it is you who need eternity...' (TM, 299) and that 'if you want to take care for your eternal future, see to it that you come to suffer for the truth... If you have loved the most beautiful girl, have lived a whole life happily with her, the most lovable wife—it cannot be recollected eternally; it is formed from what is more fragile than the eternal' (TM, 298–9).

What, then, can our *look* at de silentio's Knight of Faith—in the tax collector's exuberant stride, his dancing absorption with temporality and finitude—finally *show* us?

This question, as well as the one with which this section began— 'What does the faithful life *look* like?'—reveals a fundamental deficiency in Johannes de silentio's characterization of the faithful life: his description of the knight of faith has to do with what he imagines he might *observe* about him. Recall that de silentio's account begins with all the breathless allure of a travelogue, someone in search for that rare creature, the knight of faith: 'I have been looking for [an authentic instance of faith] for many years, but in vain. Generally, people travel around the world to see rivers and mountains, new stars, colorful birds, freakish fish, preposterous races of mankind... That does not occupy me. But if I knew where such a knight of faith lived, I would travel on foot to him, for this miracle concerns me absolutely' (FT, 32). When de silentio imagines his first sighting, he—as we well know—is astonished at his quotidian appearance: 'Dear me! Is this the person, is it actually him?—he looks just like a tax collector!' (FT, 32).

Of course, the humble *appearance* of the knight of faith is meant to indicate that a faithful person does not and cannot have some particular way of looking; the 'marvel' is not astonishing or wondrous in any conventional sense. De silentio's imaginings, however, inadvertently undermine the essential point that a faithful person does not *look* like *anything*. In fact, a person who takes up the 'light burden' of Christian faith *cannot be seen*:

> [O]nly the Christian carries—the beneficial yoke. '*My burden is light.*'
> What else is meekness except to carry the heavy burden lightly... it is
> to meekness that Christ summoned his followers: Learn from me, for

> I am meek and lowly of heart . . . Courage and high-mindedness can be
> seen, and patience can be seen in the effort, but meekness makes itself
> invisible—it *looks so light*, and yet is so heavy. That courage resides
> within is seen in the eyes . . . but *meekness cannot be seen.* (UDVS, 239–40,
> additional emphasis mine)

Kierkegaard explains the 'light' appearance of meekness with
another image: 'Just as the ship as it lightly proceeds at full sail
before the wind at the same time deeply cuts its heavy path
through the ocean, so also the Christian's way is light if one
looks at the faith that overcomes the world, but hard if one looks
at the laborious work in the depths' (UDVS, 218). The ship, as it
seems to dance over the water, is all air and sails, but the 'lightness'
of its motion is an illusion, and distracts the viewer from the actual
phenomenon of sailing: below the surface the ship is heaviness and
struggle.

Johannes de silentio's image of the dancing knight of faith, our
perambulating tax collector, is thus importantly only half of the
story: to focus on the 'dance' as *seen*, rather than as lived, is to
misunderstand the phenomenon: 'They call themselves cross-bearers
and thereby signify that their *way* through the world is *not as light as a
dance* but is heavy and hard, although faith for them is still *also* the *joy
that conquers the world*' (UDVS, 218, emphasis mine). The agility and
enthusiasm of de silentio's dancer are merely suggestive of the actual
movements of the apostolic faithful, who are understood not by those
who have seen them, but by those who conceive of them in eternal
terms:

> If someone is so enthusiastic as to consider all earthly goods as nothing,
> well, then the world is close to considering such a person mad. Yet this
> enthusiasm is not apostolic, because the apostle not only reckons the
> earthly goods as nothing, he even regards them as loss . . . nevertheless it
> is joyful, indescribably joyful, that bold confidence has the power to be
> victorious in this way . . . (UDVS, 333)

The 'bold confidence' with which the Apostles reckon loss as gain,
shame as honor, and suffering as joy is the dancer's grace rendered in
its eternal aspect; it is *this* dance that is invisible, and unavailable, to
Christendom's bureau(crat)s.

Whither Suffering?

The 'will to suffer' can now be seen as an elaboration on the theme of the Fourth Movement: the occasion of confession invites us to recognize that 'purity of heart is to will one thing': our faithful Christian striver, in pursuing her singular work in the world, will necessarily encounter all manner of challenges, from being ignored to being threatened, from partial success to abject failure. This is the kind of suffering that the faithful self relishes. It is good and necessary to grapple with the world, just as a mother delights in the pains and calamities of childbirth and child-rearing.—And here we can complete our modest comparison with canonical Buddhist thought: the Buddhist adept, through contemplative practice, is able to observe his troubles and pains, and to see them for what they actually are, the manifestations of a desirous 'self'. To see them as such is to be free of their spell: the Buddhist practitioner has groomed his mind such that the world is available to him in a non-grasping, unattached way.

So too for the Kierkegaardian faithful self: the confession, communion, and prayer that this self makes use of are practices that enable her to be in the world, existentially confident of its abundance despite the actual hardships that every vocation encounters.

These considerations, however, exist on the margins of the question we initially pursued. The 'will to suffer', as just described, is not the kind of suffering that demands an answer.

We will patiently ask the question again: how does the phenomenon of faith address the manifold misery, disaster, and horror of human life?

The answer, of course, is that it does not. Nor can it.

The question so asked is necessarily an angry one, aggrieved at what seems to be a wildly inappropriate attempt to palliate humanity's wounds. Let us return to Aleksandar Hemon's complaint: what will 'faith', even existentially rendered, do for the dying Isabel, or for her parents? Nothing, obviously; but this failure reveals a lack of conceptual fit: this question is being asked from the wrong perspective, and in the wrong way.

Life, as Kierkegaard readily avers, *is* suffering: the comportment of faith does not change that reality. What does matter is how a person inhabits her suffering. Objectively, one suffers; subjectively, the faithful person dwells within the lived practice of James: 'every gift is good and every gift is perfect'.

Objectively (that is, heard from an external, rational perspective), this latter sentiment is nonsense. Hemon is absolutely right to remark that 'Isabel's suffering and death did nothing for her, or us, or the world. We learned no lessons worth learning; we acquired no experience that could benefit anyone.'[15] What is to be done for Hemon and his family, besides genuine, useless expressions of sorrow?

'What is to be done' is the objective question. Evaluating the condition of our fellow creatures is, according to Judge William and the Jylland pastor, the ethico-religious task of every person, and attending to their needs demands our scrupulous concern. The tainted water must be cleaned up; the schoolyard bully reined in; the starving children fed and the revolution dismantled, or begun. The objective task is ongoing, and it is the work of everyone: from the PTA to the FDA, from my house to the White House, the plight of others—and ourselves—engages us in policy-making, protest, and perhaps revolt. As we saw in the Third Movement, the ethical task is never finished (and, in a sense, never gets started: the work of justifying one's choices and providing a coherent narrative of that life can never be complete).

In order to see where, and in what way, faith is made manifest, we must shift our perspective. The objective view is not, and cannot be, the subjective view.

Subjectively, only that 'single individual' understands his unique burdens; his existential grasp of what is the case *for him* is what he 'takes' with him when he engages in the practice of confession, communion, and prayer. Faith, as I have existentially and phenomenologically rendered it, is a 'heliotropic silence': a person is present to himself as he endures what he must, confident in the world's abundance, secure in his practice of faith, which turns on a central premise: 'Every good and every perfect gift is from above'. The objective view cannot see into the *aduton* of this subjective, faithful practice, and hears its utterances as, at best, a kind of prattle. Here is our tax collector as he walks the streets of Copenhagen: '... he goes past a building site

[15] Hemon (2011).

and meets another man. They talk a moment together; in no time he erects a building, having at his disposal all the resources required for that purpose. The stranger leaves him thinking he was surely a capitalist, while my admired knight thinks: "Well, if it came to that I could easily get it"' (FT, 33). The objective listener recognizes that the tax collector is a fantasist: remember, he does not have four *skillings* to his name! Subjectively, the knight of faith moves on with the confidence that he will have the resources to accomplish what *Styrelsen* demands of him in the world. This 'confidence' is not a propositional attitude; as we have seen, the James verse when entertained as a belief becomes the moment of resignation. The faithful tax collector moves forward, objectively clear-eyed about his impoverished situation, but 'quick to hear' if he is called to so build, and subjectively secure that he will have what he needs to meet that call.

The confidence of our tax collector is charming, but it draws us away from our meditation on suffering: what about when illness, crime, or, unthinkably, the death of a child, visits our blissful tax collector?

Let us consider a case of catastrophic suffering, one that will return us to the concerns often heard in the lecture hall when Kierkegaardian faith is on offer.

Giving Thanks for Fleas

The late Corrie ten Boom was a courageous survivor of World War II; she, and her family, sheltered many Jews in their Haarlem home until they were betrayed by a Dutch informant and subsequently arrested by the Gestapo. Corrie and her sister Betsie were sent to Scheveningen prison and to the Vught camp for political prisoners before ending up in the dreaded German camp Ravensbrück. In her memoir *The Hiding Place*, ten Boom reports becoming increasingly aware of Betsie's uncanny confidence and cheer in the most dire of human surroundings. When the identity of their betrayer is made known to the sisters by a new prisoner, Betsie asks Corrie to forgive him and to pray for what *he* must be suffering;[16] Betsie urges Corrie to give thanks in all

---

[16] Corrie ten Boom (1984: 305); recall the Jylland pastor's discourse in the Third Movement.

circumstances, and in particular to thank God for the crowded, fetid barracks, for the Bible they have managed to smuggle in, for their sisterly companionship, and for the fleas in their blankets. Corrie objects, and Betsie replies, 'Give thanks in all circumstances . . . It doesn't say, "in pleasant circumstances". Fleas are part of this place where God has put us.'[17] When the sisters are being processed by the barrack guards, Corrie complains that it is taking too long; Betsie answers that it may take a very long time, but 'what better way could there be to spend our lives . . . If people can be taught to hate, they can be taught to love!'[18]

Betsie ten Boom certainly resembles our faithful tax collector of the Fourth Movement. She is fully present and invested in her immediate circumstances, and in giving thanks for them; moreover, she comports herself joyfully, in an unimaginably foul setting (she even makes a joke to one of the guards about how her weak arms have slowed down her shoveling in the camp yard; the guard replies by whipping her face and neck with his leather crop).[19]

Objectively, Betsie's comportment makes no sense: fleas should be detested, betrayers and brutal guards hated. Subjectively, Betsie is dwelling in the world faithfully, and that objective evaluation is transformed by prayer and contemplative focus in the moment.

We find ourselves returning to 'Truth is Subjectivity', but with a richer sense of what is at stake for the person who lives in faith: the faithful life is a practice,[20] and a comportment, that reveals the world as infinitely available and abundant for that practitioner. Objectively, the world remains what it is, often loving and fecund, but more often sour, hostile, obdurate and always lethal. (Betsie does not survive Ravensbrück.) Subjectively, the faithful person has resources for steadfastness and joy that are not part of the objective account.

Here, at last, the wholeness of the faithful person becomes apparent. Remember that 'purity of heart is to will one thing': in his *Upbuilding Discourses in Various Spirits*, Kierkegaard warns his readers—again, using

---

[17] ten Boom (1984: 334–5).   [18] ten Boom (1984: 298).

[19] ten Boom (1984: 344).

[20] Clare Carlisle offers a wonderful meditation on the trope of motion in Kierkegaard's works; she concludes with some observations about spiritual practice and 'movement' (2005: 146–7).

a verse from the Apostle James—about the perils of being 'double-minded': '*Cleanse your hands, you sinners, and purify your hearts, you double-minded*', because only the pure in heart are able to see God and consequently to keep near to him ...' (UDVS, 24).

Why, then, is our knight of faith still riven between a rational account of his condition and a subjective experience of being in the world? The faithful knight, of course, does not suffer from 'double-mindedness', a condition that 'fears time' and 'counterfeits eternity' (UDVS, 74), because the two dimensions of his existence are indeed the same enterprise. Just as the sailing ship dances lightly over the water, 'the Christian's way is light if one looks at the faith that overcomes the world, but hard if one looks at the laborious work in the depths' (UDVS, 218): the hard labor of life can be seen as joyful, and—more to the point—faithfully experienced as 'decisive self-activity' (UDVS, 122). Rather than, say, hoisting a sail to take the prevailing wind, and then motoring in the other direction, the faithful person moves forward with 'bold confidence' (UDVS, 138) into his work in the world. This non-propositional 'confidence' is the hallmark of the faithfully navigated life: despair is gone because the faithful practitioner, in his actions, wills one thing, and is thus a whole self, rather than the divided human being that Anti-Climacus described in the First Movement.

The faithful self is whole, and able to negotiate life's vicissitudes with focused joy; despair has been banished. And what is despair? Anti-Climacus describes the despairing person as one who has not achieved the human birthright of selfhood: the 'relata' of the human condition are still at odds with each other. Kierkegaard reminds us that despair signifies something else: 'Have you reflected on what it means to despair? It means to deny that God is love!' And, to return to Kierkegaard on the wisdom of James: 'the only good and perfect gift that a human being can give is love ...' (EUD, 157).

Surely love is what faithful joy expresses, and our last turn on the Kierkegaardian dance floor will try to mete, and meet, its measure.

7

Coda

All You Need Is . . .

'[Love] connects the temporal and eternity.' (WL, 6)

Love!

Yes, that most salient, most viscerally available aspect of our tax collector has waited until now to be revealed.—Of course, love has been with us along the way, but we may now pause and remark on how, and why, the tax collector is above all a *lover*, and why it is that his loving is distinctly phenomenological in character.

Deep into his profoundly comprehensive *Works of Love*, Kierkegaard points out that it is difficult to define what it *is* to love; and so he produces an initial draft:

> Many different attempts have been made to characterize and describe how love is felt by someone in whom it is, the state of love, or what it is to love. Love has been called a feeling, a mood, a life, a passion; yet since this is such a general definition, attempts have been made to define it more precisely. Love has been called a want, but, note well, such a want that the lover continually wants what he actually possesses . . . That simple wise man of old has said, 'Love is a son of wealth and poverty.' (WL, 175)

Of course, here Kierkegaard is reminding us of Socrates' own narrative of love in the *Symposium*.[1] Since Kierkegaard does make use of this

---

[1] Cf. Johannes Climacus in the *Postscript*: 'According to Plato, Poverty and Plenty begot Eros, whose nature is made up of both. But what is existence? It is the child who is begotten by the infinite and the finite, the eternal and the temporal, and is therefore continually striving' (CUP, 1:92).

dialogue in *Works of Love* (explicitly twice,[2] with other oblique references throughout), we should remind ourselves of one account of love that Socrates is determined to correct.

Lessons in Love

The *Symposium* begins with a fairly competitive (indeed, bellicose) set of speeches about *eros*, each speaker attempting to out-do the other.[3] The speeches begin when Eryximachus repeats a remark made by Phaedrus, that Eros has been largely overlooked by the 'fancy intellectuals' and poets of the day (a combative remark, since the room is filled with fancy intellectuals). Phaedrus thus becomes the first speaker, and the first of five speeches that serve an interesting function: they provide an account of Athenian consciousness down to the present day, from the epic tales of the warrior-heroes (Phaedrus), to the creation of society with its attendant laws and artificialities (Pausanias), to the confident man of science, Eryximachus, praising the medical arts; of course, the development of the intellectual scene must also include the satirical and self-critical Aristophanic comedy, represented by Aristophanes himself; finally, Agathon brings us to the present day with the triumph of sophistical poetry (recall that he is a student of Gorgias, the famous sophist). The first set of speeches are also full of self-adulation; each speaker manages to praise himself as he sings the praises of love.[4]

Agathon (whose name, from *agathos*, means 'the good') gives a speech that marks the nadir of a gradual degeneration in the speeches. At the outset, Phaedrus reminds us, by alluding to Hesiod's *Theogony*, that Eros is among the oldest of the gods. This genealogy is suppressed when Agathon boldly claims that Eros is the most happy, beautiful,

[2] Later in *Works of Love*, Kierkegaard brings Socrates back again: 'See how that simple wise man of ancient times, who of all people knew how to speak most beautifully of the love that loves beauty and the beautiful, he was, yes, he was the ugliest man in the whole nation...' (WL, 371).

[3] In fact, Eryximachus almost bullies Phaedrus into giving the first speech, and his very proposal is somewhat hostile in its approach.

[4] Charles Salman provides a thoughtful analysis of the structure of the *Symposium* (1986).

and youngest god.[5] Of course, this is an oblique way of complimenting himself: Agathon the poet owes nothing to the archaic past: he is completely autonomous. (This suppression of the archaic past will be corrected by Socrates, who will recollect the past in the image of his own teacher, the priestess Diotima, who is herself from an archaic and mythically rich place.)

The picture of love provided by Agathon is anodyne, fit for the bathos of greeting cards: 'Love moves us to mildness, removes us from wildness. He is giver of kindness, never of meanness. Gracious, kindly . . . Treasure to lovers, envy to others, father of elegance, luxury, delicacy . . . Ornament of all gods and men, most beautiful leader and the best!'[6] Agathon is simply covering up the divisions and differences that characterize an erotic exchange; his account of love is safe, sanitized, and accordingly, empty.

Agathon's speech marks the completion of a gradual decline in the content of the speeches: he rejects the existence of violence and chaos in the presence of love; he even implies that the Symposiasts presently live in a time of friendship and peace, a denial of the war that Athens is currently conducting.

Socrates, of course, is ready to put this static, empty view of Love to the test. He asks Agathon a few questions, and arrives at this conclusion: ' . . . anyone . . . who has a desire desires what is not at hand and not present, what he does not have, and what he is not . . . for such are the objects of desire and love.'[7] *Eros* indicates lack or potential lack: you desire something that you do not have, or that you have but might lose. Therefore, *eros* cannot itself be beautiful, as Agathon claims, because *eros* is directed towards the beautiful, not towards that which it already has. The hallmark of *eros* is a condition of privation.

Kierkegaard also has much to say about the importance of need: 'Need, to have need, to be a needy person—how reluctant a person is to have this said about him! Yet we are saying the utmost when we say of the poet, "He has a need to write"; of the orator, "He has a need to speak"; and of the young woman, "She has a need to love"' (WL, 10).

This insight about 'lack' is a staple of Platonic doctrine; as Socrates is fond of reminding his audience, a yearning for what we do not know

[5] Plato (1989: 32–3).   [6] Plato (1989: 37).   [7] Plato (1989: 42).

is always preceded by a painful awareness of what it is we do not know. We must feel our need before we will be motivated to seek the remedy; as Diotima will later remark, 'A person who doesn't think of himself as lacking won't desire what he doesn't think he lacks!' (204a).[8]

Diotima's lesson is a response to the degenerate view of *eros* which reaches its final and most empty version with Agathon, who identifies himself with the god Eros; as such, Agathon is thus the youngest, most beautiful, gracious, kind, an ornament of all, the best. Agathon, the beloved of all (as Socrates ironically remarks, loved by 30,000 Greeks[9]), lacks nothing, wants nothing, desires nothing. Agathon the good (literally), Agathon the beautiful, might as well be a piece of statuary: lovely, yes, but not human.

All of the Symposiasts (with the exception of Aristophanes) focus on the feelings, the status of the beloved, rather than the lover;[10] Socrates will reverse this formulation by claiming that the beloved will become the lover. The lesson of Diotima re-introduces the notion of lack; in fact, her *eros* will be the embodiment of lack. She does not praise the beloved, but the *lover*, specifically, the lover who lacks, the lover who pursues (204c).

Need, and the passionate pursuit that it generates, is at the heart of Kierkegaard's claim that '... *this is the distinctive characteristic of love: that the one who loves by giving, infinitely, runs into infinite debt*' (WL, 177).

All You *Need* Is Love

A better sense of 'need' will surely help our analysis of Kierkegaardian need. Recall the Socratic corrective: *eros* is daimonic, dynamic: since Eros is the offspring of Poros and Penia, Resource and Need,[11] eros is both wanting and, at the same time, able to pursue what it needs. Paradoxically, the 'need' of the lover is plenitude, a want that is

---

[8] Plato (1989: 49). [9] Plato (1989: 5–6).

[10] Even Pausanias, who praises the *erastes*, the lover, turns that lover into a beloved: the lover is 'noble', 'greatly admired among men', and so forth, meaning that the lover is himself meant to be the focus of praise and admiration: the lover becomes the beloved.

[11] It is curious that Kierkegaard renders this as 'wealth and need'; resourcefulness is surely the kind of activity that Kierkegaard wants to endorse.

brimming with strategies and schemes for the care and keeping of the beloved.

Jamie Ferreira provides a clear description of Kierkegaard on need's duality: '... the need to love is generated by positive passion rather than hardship, which can be remedied. In other words, in this sense of the need of love, it is presence, rather than absence, that is the motivation.'[12] The presence of the beloved creates infinite debt: a person is never done serving, caring for, and acting on behalf of the beloved.

And who is the 'beloved'? Kierkegaard is clear on this point: '... Christian love... has only one single object, the neighbor, but the neighbor is as far as possible from being a one and only person, infinitely far from it, because the neighbor is all people' (WL, 55). Kierkegaard is not thus rejecting preferential love;[13] rather, he is describing the way in which caring for others, and their projects, is an ethical undertaking that our very nature demands. In his meditation on Matthew 22:39, 'You shall love the neighbor as yourself', Kierkegaard remarks, 'The concept "neighbor" is actually the redoubling of your own self...' (WL, 21).

How so? Ironically, Kierkegaard is making a rather Hegelian claim here. In the *Phenomenology of Spirit*'s tour de force moment that issues in 'Lordship and Bondage', we see the encounter of two conscious beings who, in the presence of the other, become *self*-conscious.[14] The basic ontological thesis is clear: a person becomes aware of herself *as* a self— and, more importantly, *becomes* the self-aware self that she is—in the presence of the other. Kierkegaard continues, '... "the neighbor" is what thinkers call "the other"...' (WL, 21), but 'the other' is thus understood as a person *like oneself*, shaped by a vast history of pains and passions, opportunity and disappointment, luck and accident, all of which is the product of a shared human community. To 'love the neighbor as your*self*' means that you must first love yourself correctly, namely, to nurture and honor the existential task given by Governance. Once 'the lock of self-love has been wrenched open' (WL, 17),

---

[12] Ferreira (2001: 21). Ferreira also points out that the word Kierkegaard uses is *Trang*, a word that indicates passionate craving.

[13] Ferreira provides a thorough examination of this complaint about Kierkegaard's corpus (2001).

[14] Hegel (1977: 111–19).

the activity of the faithful self is the realization of her vocation from moment to moment; it follows from 'appropriate self-love' that a person is obliged to honor and tend to the vocations of other persons.

This 'obligation' is two-fold. Most immediately, a person cannot be, and do, whom or what she needs to be and do without the work of others. I cannot be a professor without students, or other faculty and colleagues, nor can I do my work without classrooms (and their manifold of equipment), or without the entire institutional structure of higher education (and so forth). A person's projects are not autonomous; they are always already the projects of others. In seeing one's debt to 'the other', one also sees a deeper ontological debt (again, adumbrated by Hegel): I cannot be a person *as such* without the recognition of my fellow creatures.

Human 'Co-Constitution'

Of course, the co-constitutive nature of human being, both 'ethical' (that is, a person's characteristics and projects are always shaped by others) and 'ontological' (personhood is *essentially* created by the encounter with the other), is the thematic staple of many existential thinkers, in particular Sartre and Beauvoir. Beauvoir, in The *Ethics of Ambiguity*, makes it clear that the 'ambiguity' of our ethical relations has a Kierkegaardian lineage (Kierkegaard 'affirm[s] the irreducible character of ambiguity');[15] our human situation is 'ambiguous' in that its meaning and significance cannot be objectively fixed, but are instead continually under subjective review (given that we are always free to embrace, deny or alter our social and material conditions). 'Ambiguity' is thus Beauvoir's name for the opposed dimensions of the human constitution as described by Anti-Climacus: Beauvoir remarks, '[A human being] asserts himself as a pure internality against which no external power can take hold, and he also experiences himself as a thing crushed by the dark weight of other things.'[16] We are, says Anti-Climacus, defined by both 'possibility' and 'necessity', and at every moment a person must choose how to express that freedom in her current finite circumstance. Those choices open up

[15] Beauvoir (1997: 9).   [16] Beauvoir (1997: 7).

new possibilities, not just for the agent so choosing but for everyone else as well. This freedom, as Beauvoir puts it, is able to 'disclose being';[17] our human freedom structures the world, and furnishes it with meanings. Of course, this 'disclosing' of possibility is also part of what constitutes the persons at work in the world of their making. The 'love of the neighbor' can thus be read as a robust statement of human intersubjectivity.

The notion of human being as 'intersubjective' might lead to many important conversations,[18] but here I want to focus on 'intersubjectivity' as a specific kind of ontological observation. Heidegger's *Dasein* articulates a primordial 'being with' that always already (to use the familiar Heideggerian locution) is in, and engaged with, a world, a 'world' that is produced by the projects—and the equipment that makes those projects possible—of human society. Every human life is thus, as Heidegger puts it, 'thrown-fallen-projected being': a human infant is 'thrown' into a cultural setting, replete with language(s) and the tools that make this particular kind of life possible; that developing child 'falls' in with current coping activity, and that ongoing activity is in turn 'sighted' or guided by (Heidegger's term is *Umsicht*, 'circumspection')[19] the implicit (non-thematized) goals of that activity. As Heidegger puts it, 'One is what one does',[20] and that 'doing' happens in the cultural terrain shared by all.

Now, clearly we can, and often do, grow up and into practices that focus on our human capacity to see ourselves as rational subjects, moving through an objective environment (the text of *Being and Time* can certainly be understood in part as Heidegger's commitment to subverting this way of understanding 'human being'); we *can* see ourselves as discrete, autonomous subjects, but in so seeing ourselves we are (says Heidegger) getting the ontology wrong. 'In no case is a Dasein, untouched and unseduced by this way in which things have been interpreted, set before the open country of a "world-in-itself" so that it just beholds what it encounters.'[21] In considering how a person is to do, and be, with others (and the attendant questions of 'other

17 Beauvoir (1997: 28).
18 Cf. the work of Bataille (1962), Cixous (1979), and Levinas (1966).
19 Heidegger (1962: 98); cf. Heidegger (1982: 109, 163, 311).
20 Heidegger (1962: 283).   21 Heidegger (1962: 213).

minds'), we begin in precisely the most impoverished way if we start with a discrete self: attempts to move from an account of the 'self' to an 'other' are ultimately beached on some aporetic shore. Only 'littoral' accounts—ones that take seriously the place of human origin, neither sea nor beach, but an indeterminate and primordial oneness— can succeed in providing the conceptual apparatus for an effective phenomenology.[22] (In this regard, the very notion of 'intersubjectivity' is itself problematic: 'subjects' emerge from, and are in debt to, the cultural materials that make the 'autonomous subject' possible.) Dan Zahavi provides this elegant summation of the philosophical terrain: 'One of the quite crucial insights that we find in phenomenology is the idea that a treatment of intersubjectivity simultaneously requires an analysis of the relationship between subjectivity and world. That is, it is not possible simply to insert subjectivity somewhere within an already established ontology; rather, the three regions "self", "others", and "world" belong together; they reciprocally illuminate one another, and can only be understood in their interconnection.'[23]

To return to Kierkegaard: the 'need' that characterizes human life is evidently an expression of this ontological reality. Kierkegaard claims that 'Love is not a being-for-itself quality but a quality by which or in which you are for others' (WL, 223); the need to love and the debt thus incurred is, when correctly acknowledged and acted upon, a recognition that human beings are intersubjectively consti- tuted. This 'need' that Kierkegaard extols is, as we just observed, not merely a call to care for the neighbor because it is morally or Chris- tianly demanded (although this is certainly the case); at its fundamen- tal level, 'need' is an expression of the human condition: we are who we are in the presence of others. Again, the exhortation to 'love the neighbor as yourself' is thus no mere heuristic, prompting us to think beyond the 'black box' of the self with its careful record of private systems and operations; instead, 'the love of the neighbor' acknow- ledges how it is that we, and the world we share, *really are*. The fabric of

[22] Cf. Frater Taciturnus's description of the lake from which he claims to dredge up the manuscript of 'Guilty?'/'Not Guilty?': 'The lake is not easy to approach, for it is surrounded by a rather wide stretch of quagmire. Here the boundary dispute between the lake and the land goes on night and day' (SLW, 187).

[23] Zahavi (2001: 166).

the world—to be precise, the fabric of Spirit—is thus, and we ignore this reality and its demands at our peril: 'It is only in love for the neighbor that the self, who loves, is defined as spirit purely spiritually and the neighbor is a purely spiritual specification' (WL, 56–7), 'spirit' here understood as the shared habits and practices in which we dwell, and that ultimately make our lives possible. The more clearly we see our intersubjective debt, the better we will be able to do our work in the world—work that is made possible (or indeed thwarted) by others.

All You Need Is *Love*

Human beings are intersubjectively co-constituting; this is why, as Kierkegaard puts it, 'Love builds up' (WL, 212). Here Kierkegaard has in mind *opbyggelig*, the 'upbuilding' that characterizes many of his religious discourses; however, he also wants his readers to attend to the metaphorical implications of 'building up'. As he puts it: 'Everyone who builds does build, but not everyone who builds does build up. For example, when a man is building a wing on his house we do not say that he is building up a wing but that he is building on . . . to build up is to erect something *from the ground up*' (WL, 210–11). And what is this structure like? The foundation of this dwelling is love, and its upbuilding work is also love: 'In every human being in whom there is love, the foundation, in the spiritual sense, is laid. And the building that, in the spiritual sense, is to be erected is again love . . . ' Furthermore, this activity is available to all of us, at all times: 'At every moment there lives a countless throng of people; it is possible that everything that any human being undertakes, everything that any human being says, can be upbuilding . . . ' (WL, 215).

Here the 'house' metaphor is perhaps misleading; as the previous quote suggests, we should focus on the dynamic *activity* of building itself. Love, as Kierkegaard insistently reminds us, is 'sheer action': ' . . . Christian love . . . is whole and collected, present in its every expression, and yet it is sheer action; consequently it is as far from inaction as it is from busyness. It never accepts anything in advance or gives a promise in place of action; it never rests satisfied in the delusion of being finished; it never dwells indulgently on itself . . . Christian love is sheer action, and its every work is holy, because it is the fulfilling of the Law' (WL, 98–9).

Hence, *works* of love: the faithful striver is always immersed in the task of loving, always engaged in care of and concern for the neighbor.

We are now ready to return to the erotic lesson of Diotima. Recall Agathon's static picture of Love as a pretty and posing beloved object: Socrates reintroduces the need that necessarily characterizes love. Diotima, as Socrates tells his listeners, was quick to correct his own thinking about the nature of love, and thus we move from the fixed and sterile portrait of Agathon to one that is dynamic and engaged: Diotima likens love in all of its forms to pregnancy. Eros, she argues, is not itself beautiful, nor does it ultimately want the beautiful: what Love wants is to *give birth*, or bring forth, in the presence of that which it finds beautiful. What we want is immortality, and we get it through different kinds of 'procreation': a person perpetuates herself by replicating and regenerating herself.

Diotima thus describes human life as a profound expression of our intersubjective debt. Consider the origin and development of any *Livs-anskuelse*, life-view: imagine a child hearing a passage of poetry that sounds incredibly moving and beautiful: she goes to the library to find this poem, and thus begins a passion. She studies the poem, she recites it to others, perhaps she writes an essay about it, or even writes poems that resemble it: suddenly the child is no longer simply a lover of that poem. By admiring its beauty, she wanted to become more familiar with it, and that familiarity prompted her to emulate it, to imitate it: and thus she herself reproduces its beauty in a form of her own making.

A pregnant woman is said to be 'expecting'; Kierkegaard often remarks that the faithful person lives in expectancy: 'To expect contains within itself the same duality that the possible has, and to expect is to relate oneself to the possible ... ' (WL, 249). Abraham, the 'father-in-waiting', is the paradigm of being expectant: 'Abraham, though grey-haired, was young enough to wish to be a father. Outwardly, the wonder is that it happened in accordance with their expectation; in a deeper sense, the wonder of faith consists in Abraham and Sarah being young enough to wish and in faith's having preserved their wish and with it their youth' (FT, 15). Yes, their youth! The long gestation of their promised task is borne out not in a disappointed old age, but in joyful enthusiasm. Kierkegaard remarks, ' ... a person's whole life should be the time of hope!' (WL, 251). The faithful person, immersed in his tasks and projects, is always ready for the good: not as a wish, but as the material possibility for the expression and creation of good works.

This readiness is, most importantly, not simply for one's own projects: in being receptive to the possibilities for the good, a person is always already receptive to, and ready to act upon, the good for others. Again, the ontological point is clear: 'love' is relational, and any desire for the success of one's work in the world is, when seen correctly, a wish for the success of others. Kierkegaard remarks, 'No one can hope unless he is also loving; he cannot *hope for himself* without also being loving, because the good has an infinite connectedness; but if he is loving, he also hopes for others' (WL, 255). This is why there is, for the faithful striver, '...a task at every moment' (WL, 189); in loving openness to what is actually the case, the faithful person (guided, of course, by the wisdom of James) is ready to act, ready to participate: the faithful person is ready to love.

The Tax Collector: Love's Revolutionary

'Love is a revolution, the most profound of all, but the most blessed!... love...is a revolution from the ground up.' (WL, 265–6)

So! Our enigmatic, ecstatic, absorbed and joyful tax collector is, above all, a lover, and in a profoundly ontological sense: he understands the need for the other, and the debt such bonds necessarily create, and the action thus called for, at all times. And so he must perambulate, taking in his surroundings, from moment to moment, always available to his 'neighbor' and to his environment at large. The tax collector understands—faithfully, not thematically or by means of a set of beliefs—that he is responsible for the conditions that currently surround him.

And what of him?

Now is the time to watch him amble out of sight, on to his next building project or delight-filled dinner: the tax collector's happy strolling, when observed (or imagined, as the fictional Johannes de silentio does), cannot teach us very much; his attentive delight in each moment conceals the work that makes his life possible.

And yet: I am still intrigued by him. Why?

Surely it is because his cheer beckons me, and issues me an invitation. The summons is quite specific: I am called to leave his absorbed and joyful silence and to begin listening again, and again, to the many voices that need to be heard. As I write, as I teach, as I love and live with my family and my friends, the promise of this depiction of lived practice stays with me. The tax collector is a compelling figure—an image, nothing more—but one that always renews my conviction that the life of a self forged in faith is the only life worth living, or—more to the point—*worthy* of being lived.

A Wendell Berry poem comes to mind:

> Learn by little the desire for all things
> which perhaps is not desire at all
> but undying love which perhaps
> is not love at all but gratitude
> for the being of all things which
> perhaps is not gratitude at all
> but the maker's joy in what is made,
> the joy in which we come to rest.[24]

Or, perhaps—to follow in the footsteps of our blissfully sauntering knight of faith—the joy in which we move through the world, one we ourselves co-constitute, from moment to gloriously loving moment.

---

[24] Wendell Berry (2010: 99).

8

A First And Last Explanation

For the sake of form and order, I hereby acknowledge what is surely of little interest to the reader: I, Sheridan Hough, am civilly and legally responsible for this text.[1] The narrative voice, however, is not my own; the typescript is mine, but it is not my typing. I have merely played the role of a prompter, coaxing the poetic voice to stand up and have her say. The author of this work, known hereafter as 'Sheridan Hough, Lover of the Tax Collector' ('SH, LTC'), has taken a singular path through the vast mansions of Magister Kierkegaard's corpus, one that I have considered with some interest. It seems to me that she has faithfully—pun intended—followed the trail of the elusive Tax Collector (and he only a seeming, and indeed one of de silentio's own) through the Kierkegaardian estates. And as for her conclusions? Dear Reader—if I may presume to have one—I leave this analysis entirely to you. One reader has already observed that this 'account' of suffering may indeed underscore Bishop Martensen's point, that Kierkegaard's Christianity demands extreme situations well beyond the usual strains and frustrations of ordinary life. I cannot offer an answer here, but will only observe, as Johannes Climacus remarks, that I have ' . . . no qualification for being a party liner, because I have no opinion except that it must be the most difficult of all to become a Christian' (CUP, 1: 619).

There is no doubt: 'SH, LTC' has a definite life-view, and indeed one with which I have become quite familiar. But a warning must again be issued: let this person speak for herself. To borrow a phrase from the Magister's own explanation of his work: I hope that no reader is fooled (or fools herself) into thinking that *my* 'personal actuality' is on the scene, rather than, as Kierkegaard puts it,

---

[1] For Kierkegaard's 'First and Last Explanation', see CUP, 1:625.

'... the light, doubly reflected ideality of a poetically actual author to dance with...' (CUP, 1: 628). Indeed. And dancing is often pleasant, when tune and temper are in good order. So! I trust that your time on the dance floor with 'SH, LTC' has at least been agreeable; your philosophical judgment is, of course, another matter.

And with this I take leave of her. If, in future, it should occur to anyone to quote from, or refer to, this document, it is my wish that this person cite the name of 'SH, LTC'—not mine. Of course, I do not shirk my civil and scholarly responsibility for this construction, and I will do my best to answer questions (and indeed grievances) from my role as secretary. Insofar as 'SH, LTC' may have affronted or offended any respectable person, in any way, particularly those persons I admire, I hereby make my apology to them. I suppose I can do no better for this poetic voice, and her conclusions, than to remind the reader of Magister Kierkegaard's own indecision about revealing his authorship: in his journal he remarked, 'But no! I owe it to the truth ... to do everything as has been decided, leaving the outcome up to God and accepting everything from his hand as a good and perfect gift...' (JP 5, 5872). 'SH, LTC' may welcome this valedictory, or not; I do not have an opinion in the matter. I do, however, ardently wish that her words will be permitted to stand in the spirit she offers them.

Sheridan Hough
2015

Bibliography

Aristotle. 1996. *The Politics and The Constitution of Athens*, 2nd ed., trans. Stephen Everson. Cambridge: Cambridge University Press.

Augustine. 1961. *Confessions*, trans. R.S. Pine-Coffin, New York: Penguin Books.

Bataille, Georges. 1962. *Death and Sensuality: A Study of Eroticism and the Taboo*. New York: Walker and Company.

Bauckham, James. 1999. *Wisdom of James, Disciple of Jesus the Sage*. London and New York: Routledge.

Berry, Wendell. 2010. *Leavings: Poems*. Berkeley: Counterpoint Press.

Carlisle, Clare. 2005. *Kierkegaard's Philosophy of Becoming: Movements and Positions*. New York: SUNY Press.

Cixous, Hélène. 1979. *Vivre l'orange/To live the orange*, bilingual ed., trans. Ann Liddle and Sarah Cornell. Paris: Des Femmes.

Cixous, Hélène. 1986 [1975]. *Sorties*. In *The Newly Born Woman* by Hélène Cixous and Catherine Clement, trans. Betsy Wing. Manchester: Manchester University Press.

Clark, Maudmarie. 1990. *Nietzsche on Truth and Philosophy*. Cambridge: Cambridge University Press.

Coseru, Christian. 2012. *Perceiving Reality: Consciousness, Intentionality, and Cognition in Buddhist Philosophy*. Oxford: Oxford University Press.

Davenport, John J., and Rudd, Anthony, eds. 2001. *Kierkegaard After MacIntyre*. Peru: Open Court Publishing.

Davidson, Donald. 1980. 'How is Weakness of the Will Possible?' *Essays on Actions and Events*, 21–42. New York: Oxford University Press.

de Beauvoir, Simone. 1997. *The Ethics of Ambiguity*, trans. Bernard Frechtman. Secaucus: Carol Publishing Group.

Dewey, Bradley Rau. 1967. 'Kierkegaard and the Blue Testament.' *Harvard Theological Review* 60: 391–409.

Dostoyevsky, Fyodor. 1950. *The Brothers Karamazov*, trans. Constance Garnett. New York: Random House.

Dreyfus, Hubert. 1991. *Being-in-the-World: A Commentary on Heidegger's Being and Time, Division I*. Cambridge, MA: The MIT Press.

Evans, C. Stephen. 2004. *Kierkegaard's Ethic of Love: Divine Commands and Moral Obligations*. Oxford: Oxford University Press.

Evans, C. Stephen. 2006. 'Is Kierkegaard an Irrationalist?' *Kierkegaard on Faith and the Self*, 117–32. Waco: Baylor University Press.

Ferreira, M. Jaimie. 2001. *Love's Grateful Striving: A Commentary on Kierkegaard's Works of Love*. Oxford: Oxford University Press.

Feyerabend, Paul. 1995. *Killing Time*. Chicago: The University of Chicago Press.

Gibson, J.J. 1979. *The Ecological Approach to Visual Perception*. Boston: Houghton Mifflin.

Glenn Jr., John D. 1987. 'The Definition of the Self and the Structure of Kierkegaard's Work.' *International Kierkegaard Commentary: The Sickness Unto Death*. Robert L. Perkins, ed., 5–21. Macon, GA: Mercer University Press.

Hannay, Alastair. 1987. 'Spirit and the Idea of the Self as a Reflexive Relation.' *International Kierkegaard Commentary: The Sickness Unto Death*. Robert L. Perkins, ed., 23–38. Macon, GA: Mercer University Press.

Hannay, Alastair. 2001. *Kierkegaard: A Biography*. Cambridge: Cambridge University Press.

Hegel, G.W.F. 1977. *Phenomenology of Spirit*, trans. A.V. Miller. Oxford: Oxford University Press.

Heidegger, Martin. 1962. *Being and Time*, trans. J. Macquarrie and E. Robinson. New York: Harper and Row.

Heidegger, Martin. 1968. *What Is Called Thinking?*, trans. J. Glenn Gray and Fred W. Wieck. New York: Harper and Row.

Heidegger, Martin. 1982. *The Basic Problems of Phenomenology*, trans. Richard Polt and Albert Hofstadter. Bloomington: Indiana University Press.

Heidegger, Martin. 1986. *Sein und Zeit*. Tübingen: Max Niemeyer.

Hemon, Aleksandar. 'The Aquarium.' *The New Yorker*, June 13, 2011.

Hough, Sheridan. 1997. *Nietzsche's Noontide Friend: The Self as Metaphoric Double*. University Park, PA: Pennsylvania State University Press.

Hough, Sheridan. 2005. ' "Halting is Movement": the Paradoxical Pause of Confession in "An Occasional Discourse",' in Robert L. Perkins, ed., *Upbuilding Discourses in Various Spirits, International Kierkegaard Commentary*, vol. 15, Macon, GA: Mercer University Press.

Hough, Sheridan. 2007. 'What the Faithful Tax Collector Saw (Against the Understanding),' in Robert L. Perkins, ed., *Without Authority, International Kierkegaard Commentary*, vol. 18, Macon, GA: Mercer University Press.

Hough, Sheridan. 2009. 'The Bureau(crat), the Dancer, and the Movements of Faithful Self-Concern,' in Robert L. Perkins, ed., *The Moment and Late Writings, International Kierkegaard Commentary*, vol. 23, Macon, GA: Mercer University Press.

Hough, Sheridan. 2010. 'Silence, "Composure in Existence," and the Promise of Faith's Joy,' in Marc A. Jolley, ed., *Why Kierkegaard Matters*, Macon, GA: Mercer University Press.

Husserl, Edmund. 1969. *Zur Phänomenologie des inneren Zeitbewusstseins* (1893–1917). Rudolf Boehm, ed., The Hague: Martinus Nijhoff.

Husserl, Edmund. 1970. *The Crisis of the European Sciences and Transcendental Phenomenology: An Introduction to Phenomenological Philosophy*, trans. David Carr. Evanston, IL: Northwestern University Press.

Husserl, Edmund. 1977. *Cartesian Meditations: An Introduction to Phenomenology*, trans. D. Cairns. Dordrecht: Kluwer Academic Publishers.

Husserl, Edmund. 1989. *Ideas: General Introduction to Pure Phenomenology and to a Phenomenological Philosophy* 2, trans. R. Rojcewicz and A. Schuwer. Dordrecht: Kluwer Academic Publishers.

Husserl, Edmund. 1991. *On the Phenomenology of the Consciousness of Internal Time* (1893–1917), Collected Works, Volume 4, trans. John Barnett Brough, ed. Martin Heidegger. The Hague; Kluwer Academic Publishers.

Kant, Immanuel. 1965. *Critique of Pure Reason*, trans. Norman Kemp Smith. New York: St. Martin's Press.

Kierkegaard, Søren. 1938. *Purity of Heart is To Will One Thing*, trans. Douglas V. Steere. New York: Harper and Row Publishers.

Kierkegaard, Søren. 1962. *The Present Age*, trans. Alexander Dru. New York: Harper Torchbooks.

Kierkegaard, Søren. 1967–1978. *Søren Kierkegaard's Journals and Papers*, 1–7, ed. and trans. Howard V. Hong and Edna H. Hong, assisted by Gregor Malantschuk. Bloomington and London: Indiana University Press.

Kierkegaard, Søren. 1978. *Two Ages: the Age of Revolution and the Present Age*, trans. Howard V. Hong and Edna H. Hong. Princeton: Princeton University Press.

Kierkegaard, Søren. 1980. *The Concept of Anxiety*, trans. Reidar Thomte in collaboration with Albert B. Anderson. Princeton: Princeton University Press.

Kierkegaard, Søren. 1980. *The Sickness Unto Death*, trans. Howard V. Hong and Edna H. Hong. Princeton: Princeton University Press.

Kierkegaard, Søren. 1982. *The Concept of Irony*, trans. Howard V. Hong and Edna H. Hong. Princeton: Princeton University Press.

Kierkegaard, Søren. 1983. *Repetition*, trans. Howard V. Hong and Edna H. Hong. Princeton: Princeton University Press.

Kierkegaard, Søren. 1985. *Philosophical Fragments and 'Johannes Climacus*, trans. Howard H. Hong and Edna H. Hong. Princeton: Princeton University Press.

Kierkegaard, Søren. 1987. *Either/Or*, vols. 1–2, trans. Howard V. Hong and Edna H Hong. Princeton: Princeton University Press.

Kierkegaard, Søren. 1988. *Stages on Life's Way*, trans. Howard V. Hong and Edna H. Hong. Princeton: Princeton University Press.

Kierkegaard, Søren. 1990. *Early Polemical Writings*, trans. Julia Watkin. Princeton: Princeton University Press.

Kierkegaard, Søren. 1990. *Eighteen Upbuilding Discourses*, trans. Howard V. Hong and Edna H. Hong. Princeton: Princeton University Press.

Kierkegaard, Søren. 1991. *Practice in Christianity*, trans. Howard V. Hong and Edna H. Hong. Princeton: Princeton University Press.

Kierkegaard, Søren. 1992. *Concluding Unscientific Postscript to 'Philosophical Fragments*,' two vols., trans. Howard V. Hong and Edna H. Hong. Princeton: Princeton University Press.

Kierkegaard, Søren. 1993. *Upbuilding Discourses in Various Spirits*, trans. Howard V. Hong and Edna H. Hong. Princeton: Princeton University Press.

Kierkegaard, Søren. 1995. *Works of Love*, trans. Howard V. Hong and Edna H. Hong. Princeton: Princeton University Press.

Kierkegaard, Søren. 1997. *Without Authority*, trans. Howard V. Hong and Edna H. Hong. Princeton: Princeton University Press.

Kierkegaard, Søren. 1998. *The Moment and Late Writings*, trans. Howard V. Hong and Edna H. Hong. Princeton: Princeton University Press.

Kierkegaard, Søren. 1998. *The Point of View for My Work as an Author*, trans. Howard V. Hong and Edna H. Hong. Princeton: Princeton University Press.

Kierkegaard, Søren. 2006. *Fear and Trembling*, trans. Sylvia Walsh. Cambridge: Cambridge University Press.

Kirmmse, Bruce H. 1990. *Kierkegaard in Golden Age Denmark*. Bloomington and Indianapolis: Indiana University Press.

Law, David. 1996. 'The Place, Role and Function of the "Ultimatum" of Either/Or, Part Two, in Kierkegaard's Pseudonymous Writings,' in *International Kierkegaard Commentary: Either/Or, II*. Robert Perkins, ed., 233–59. Macon, GA: Mercer University Press.

Léon, Céline, and Walsh, Sylvia, eds. 1997. *Feminist Interpretations of Søren Kierkegaard*. University Park, PA: Pennsylvania State Press.

Léon, Céline. 2008. *The Neither/Nor of the Second Sex: Kierkegaard on Women, Sexual Difference, and Sexual Relations*. Macon, GA: Mercer University Press.

Levinas, Emmanuel. 1966. *Basic Philosophical Writings*. Adriaan T. Peperzak, Simon Critchley, Robert Bernasconi, eds. Bloomington: Indiana University Press.

Lippitt, John. 2003. *Kierkegaard and Fear and Trembling*. London and New York: Routledge.

Merleau-Ponty, Maurice. 1962. *The Phenomenology of Perception*, trans. Colin Smith. London: Routledge and Kegan Paul.

Molbech, Christian. 1859. *Dansk Ordbog* (2 vols.). Copenhagen: F. Hegel.

Mooney, Edward F. 1991. *Knights of Faith and Resignation: Reading Kierkegaard's Fear and Trembling*. Albany: State University of New York Press.

Morris, Richard. 1989–1995. *The Aṅguttara-Nikāya*. Vols. I–II. The Pali Text Society. London: Luzac.

Nietzsche, Friedrich. 1961. *Thus Spoke Zarathustra*, trans. R.J. Hollingdale. New York: Penguin Books.

Nietzsche, Friedrich. 1980. *Sämtliche Werke: Kritische Studienausgabe in 15 Bänden*. Giorgio Collini and Mazzino Montinari, eds. Berlin: de Gruyter.

Nietzsche, Friedrich. 1983. *Untimely Meditations*, trans. R.J. Hollingdale. Cambridge: Cambridge University Press.

Nietzsche, Friedrich. 1998. *On the Genealogy of Morality*, trans. Maudemarie Clark and Alan J. Swensen. Indianapolis: Hackett Publishing Company.

Pattison, George. 2002. *Kierkegaard's Upbuilding Discourses: Philosophy, Literature and Theology*. London and New York: Routledge.

Pattison, George. 2005. *The Philosophy of Kierkegaard*. Montreal: McGill-Queen's University Press.

Perkins, Robert. 1973. 'Kierkegaard's Epistemological Preferences.' *International Journal for Philosophy of Religion* 4 (4): 197–217.

Perkins, Robert. 1990. 'Kierkegaard, A Kind of Epistemologist.' *History of European Ideas* 12 (1): 7–18.

Perkins, Robert. 2007. *International Kierkegaard Commentary: Without Authority*. Robert Perkins, ed. Macon, GA: Mercer University Press.

Piety, M.G. 2010. *Ways of Knowing: Kierkegaard's Pluralist Epistemology*. Waco: Baylor University Press.

Plato, 1987. *Gorgias*, trans. Donald J. Zeyl. Indianapolis: Hackett Publishing Company.

Plato, 1989. *Symposium*, trans. Alexander Nehamas and Paul Woodruff. Indianapolis: Hackett Publishing Company.

Poole, Roger. 1998. 'The Unknown Kierkegaard: Twentieth-Century Receptions,' *The Cambridge Companion to Kierkegaard*, Cambridge: Cambridge University Press.

Salman, Charles. 1986. *The Contrivance of Eros in Plato's Symposium*. Ph.D. thesis, Yale University.

Sartre, Jean-Paul. 1956. *Being and Nothingness*, trans. Hazel Barnes. New York: Washington Square Press.

Siegel, Susanna. 2010. *The Contents of Visual Experience*. Oxford: Oxford University Press.

Solomon, Robert. 1983. *In the Spirit of Hegel*. Oxford: Oxford University Press.

Stewart, Jon. 2003. *Kierkegaard's Relations to Hegel Reconsidered*. Cambridge: Cambridge University Press.

Taylor, Charles. 1985. *Human Agency and Language, Philosophical Papers I*. Cambridge: Cambridge University Press.

ten Boom, Corrie. 1984. *The Hiding Place*. Grand Rapids: Baker Publishing Group.

Walsh, Sylvia. 1994. *Living Poetically: Kierkegaard's Existential Aesthetics*. University Park, PA: Pennsylvania State University Press.

Walsh, Sylvia. 2005. *Living Christianly: Kierkegaard's Dialectic of Christian Existence*. University Park, PA: Pennsylvania State University Press.

Westphal, Merold. 1996. *Becoming a Self: A Reading of Kierkegaard's Concluding Unscientific Postscript*. West Lafayette: Purdue University Press.

Yeats, William Butler. 1996. *The Collected Poems of W.B. Yeats*. Richard Finnernan, ed. New York: Simon and Schuster.

Zahavi, Dan. 2001. 'Beyond Empathy.' *Between Ourselves: Second-Person Issues in the Study of Consciousness, Journal of Consciousness Studies 8*, no. 5–7.

Index